LIFE IN EXILE: A JOURNEY HOME

BASIC EDITION

50 YEARS OF MUSIC FROM THE BAND

EXILE

EVE NICOLE LEMAIRE

For Pop

and Steven

ACKNOWLEDGEMENTS

I would like to thank, first and foremost, my mom, for teaching me how to write the alphabet when I was only two or three years old. You always told me I could do anything I wanted to do, and I love you dearly. Next, I would like to thank everyone who agreed to be interviewed for this book. Exile deserved for their story to be told, and thank you so much for helping me to make that happen. I would especially like to thank Steven for being my biggest supporter. You always knew I could do it! Finally, I would like to thank my friends for cheering me on along the way: Tash, Carter, Promila, Martha, Will, Bakar, George, Toni, Jim and Lois, you guys are great! And speaking of Lois, thank you for all of your help with formatting. I couldn't have done this without you.

INTRO

My first real memory of seeing Exile is from their '78 tour opening up for Aerosmith at Rupp Arena in Lexington, KY. There were so many people backstage, so much excitement. It was electrifying. Right before he was to go on, my dad took me up onstage and placed me in front of a huge stack of Marshall amps. That wall of amps towered over me as I sat cross-legged, waiting for them to go on. I had seen my dad play hundreds of times in clubs all across the country in my seven young years, but never before had he been in an arena setting, as part of a #1-record-selling band, who just happened to be opening for Aerosmith.

After what seemed like an eternity, a man's deep voice announced "Welcome to Rupp Arena! And put your hands together for Kentucky's own... Exile!" The lights went up, the crowd cheered like wild, and there they were in all their 70's rock-n-roll glory. My dad started thumping out those instantly recognizable bass notes to their hit "Kiss You All Over," *Bum, bum, bum, bu-um bum bum.* Next, Buzz and Marlon came in with the synth, and the crowd was going crazy. Jimmy, in his trademark red spandex pants, shook his long hair back and forth and sang out in his amazing raspy-dreamy voice: "When I get home babe, gonna light your fire..." and the whole thing was just magic. Like I said, I had watched my dad play shows all my life, but it had always been in smaller clubs and bars. Sure, I'd seen crowds go wild, but I had never been to a packed stadium show like this, listening to the deafening roar of the crowd. There is nothing like it in the world to be on stage watching the people you love make amazing music and holding the crowd in the palm of their hands. It's powerful stuff.

Meanwhile, dad's bass line was thumping through the monster stack of amps, *Bum, bu-um bum bum.* I could feel the beat from the massive amps pounding all the way through my chest. *Bum, bu-um bum bum.* The sound was shaking my whole body. It felt like a gong pounding right through my ribcage, like my heart was the bass beat and it was going to thump right out of my body. I started to sweat. I felt a little dizzy. Wait! This wasn't right. This was my dad's big night! The whole band's big night, opening for one of the greatest rock-n-roll bands ever! I tried my best not to think about it; to relax, sit back, and listen to the music, but that thumping just wouldn't stop. I felt full-on nauseous. Next thing I knew I leaned over... and puked.

Now THAT'S rock-n-roll.

At this point my mom swooped down, picked me up, cleaned me off, and took me to my grandmother's house. My grandmother gave me a cold washcloth for my head and told me to lie still. Slowly, the dizziness subsided. I was fine, of course, but I never got to see Exile finish their big set, or to see Aerosmith. But it was on that night that I realized how truly powerful music can be. And also, you probably shouldn't sit your kid in front of a stack of Marshall amps. But hey, I had music in my blood.

So, that's my story. And now I'd like to share some of the amazing history of Kentucky's own Exile (or The Exiles, as they were called back in the day). This year they are celebrating 50 years as a band. 50 years! Think about it: the Rolling Stones just celebrated their 50 years together in

2012. Of course, Exile never quite achieved the same level of fame as the Stones, but their fans will tell you that they put on a helluva live show. In fact, they have always been about the live performance. In talking to past and present band members, roadies, friends and fans, one thing that always came up was their live show. The various members of Exile have always put on a great, professional, full of heart-and-soul performance (except for that one disastrous time at the Opry, but I'll get to that later).

This is not an exhaustive, minute-by-minute history of Exile. It is simply a story about a great group of guys from a small part of the world who just happened to make it big. And it's also a little bit about my journey as the daughter of one of those guys.

But, enough about me.

THE BEGINNING

Anyone at all familiar with Exile knows that the band has had a rotating cast of characters since its inception. But who were the very first members way back in 1963? Well, that's an interesting story. The 60s was an amazing time for music, even in rural central Kentucky, and especially in Richmond and Lexington, two of Kentucky's big college towns. R&B was a really popular genre, and the nascent British Invasion was starting to filter into mainstream music, inspiring young musicians everywhere to form bands of their own. At that time there were many venues all around the region in which to see live music. Some clubs even hosted a teen night, so kids in junior high and high school were able to see and participate in the local live music scene.

In 1962 a group of mostly high school kids from Madison High School and Madison Central in Richmond, KY decided to form a band called The Fascinations: Doug Jones, Billy Luxon, Paul Smith, Jr, Ernie Rhodus, Ronnie Hall, Jimmy Stokley and Mack Davenport were in that band. Billy Luxon was in the senior high school concert band when he met a young fellow named Buzz Cornelison, a freshman. Buzz played piano so well that he was asked to join the senior concert band, and it was there that Billy and Buzz got to know one another. Like many high school bands, the Fascinations practiced a lot, but in actuality they played very few gigs.

A year later in 1963, after he had already graduated, Billy came back and found Buzz in their same old high school band room and told him that the Fascinations were changing up their presentation and format. They were scrapping The Fascinations and starting a new band called The Exiles. The story goes that Mack Davenport had read a book about Cuban refugees living in exile after the 1959 Cuban revolution, and he thought that "The Exiles" would be a good name for their new band. About the name change Billy Luxon recalled:

> We felt like exiles anyway, because at that point in time nobody in Richmond, KY had long hair or wore any type of clothes that were out of the ordinary, so we really were, I guess, in that day, we were kinda

outcasts. So "Exiles" became a really appropriate name.

Neither Ernie Rhodus nor Doug Jones made the change from the Fascinations to The Exiles, and there is some amount of debate as to whether or not Ronnie Hall did, either. Some of the original band members say that Ronnie did continue on and was in The Exiles for a short period, and that he and Jimmy Stokley briefly shared lead vocals; others say that they shared vocals in the Fascinations, but when the change was made to The Exiles, Jimmy Stokley was their sole lead singer.

At that time, local bands didn't perform original music - they were all cover bands. The Exiles did a lot of R&B: James Brown, the Temptations, the Four Tops, and with both Ronnie and Stokley on vocals they could do a wide variety of songs. Ronnie had a smooth, refined voice, and Stokley had a low growl. A few months later, however, Ronnie joined the National Guard and left the band for good. Stokley then became the sole lead singer for the band. Again, there is some discrepancy as to whether or not this joint effort occurred during the Fascinations or The Exiles.

Despite this debate, the rest of the lineup is certain: Billy Luxon played trumpet and sang background vocals; Mike Howard played guitar, and Paul Smith, Jr played bass; Mack Davenport was on drums, and all they needed now was a keyboard player. Billy came back that day to find Buzz to ask him if would join their new band. Buzz replied, "But I don't have a keyboard." Billy then told him that Jimmy Stokley had bought one in the hopes that he could play, but it hadn't worked out too well, so if he wanted to Buzz could play that one.

Being just 15 years old at the time, Buzz had to ask for his parents' permission, so he went home for dinner that evening and asked his parents if he could join the band. He said his father "gave him a sanguine look," because ever since the 4th grade, all little Buzzy had ever wanted to do was act. At the urging of his aunt, who was in the local theatre group, he had taken piano lessons so that he could have a direction for his creativity. He played piano and keyboard for enjoyment, but his true passion was for the theatre. That same aunt happened to be over for dinner that fateful evening, and she convinced his parents that this would be a good creative outlet for him, since he had always wanted to be on the stage. Due to his tender years, his parents had to drive him to his first band practice in Richmond, which took place in Mike Howard's basement. Thereafter, his band mates would have to come get him to take him to shows and rehearsals, because he was still too young to drive.

At that first rehearsal Buzz remembered how nice everyone was, and that they all got along really well. It was then that he met Mack Davenport for the first time. Everyone else was chatty and excited, but Mack stayed quiet and didn't speak to him at all. Buzz would make a comment or ask a question, and Mack would just look at him. Buzz decided to break the ice by saying something nice and complimenting Mack directly, but all he could think of to say was:

Buzz: "That's a really nice drum set."

Mack: "Thank you very much."

Silence.

They didn't speak again for the rest of practice.

Buzz left the rehearsal thinking Mack hated him. "This is never going to work," he feared. But at the next rehearsal, Mack talked to him like they had known each other all their lives. It seemed this band of exiles just might work out, after all.

Buzz's story bears some distinct similarities to the next member added to the band, Jimmy "J.P." Pennington (Note: since Jimmy Stokley and Jimmy Pennington are both named "Jimmy," to avoid any confusion from here on out Jimmy Pennington will be referred to as J.P., and Jimmy Stokley as Stokley). J.P. was a talented young guitarist who was playing in a band with his cousins with Clyde "Red" Foley ("Peace in the Valley," "Chattanooga Shoe Shine Boy"), a renowned country artist from Berea. But, his cousins' band had needed a bass player, not a guitarist, so J.P. managed to modify his guitar to play bass with them. One day J.P. was out mowing his front yard when Billy and Stokley pulled up in Stokley's '59 blue Pontiac, the model with the fins. It was, by all accounts, a great car, and the locals knew it on sight. Billy and Stokley had heard around town that J.P. was quite a good guitarist, and they wanted him to join their new band.

For those who don't know, Stokley was somewhat of a local character. He was known as a wild dancer and a ladies man. He would be the first to get out on the dance floor and do the The Alligator, a dance which required a person to flop down on his back and wave his arms and legs spasmodically in the air. Considered by high school administrators to be subversive, it was outlawed at practically every school dance in the region. Jimmy was unceremoniously asked to leave a school dance on one such occasion when he went against protocol and decided to get down and do The Alligator anyway, thus cementing his reputation. In addition, he also had long hair down to his rear. Everything about him exuded bad boy and cool guy.

For Stokley to come and seek out J.P. to be in a band was a compliment indeed. Not to mention the fact that, like Buzz, J.P. was also a kid - a mere 14 years old. Stokley and Billy were a good three to five years older than he, and between the car and the cool older guys, how could he say no? But in the end he, too, had to ask his folks for permission. J.P. said his parents didn't take his request to play with a bunch of local kids too seriously, but they consented nonetheless. Like Buzz, J.P.'s dad also had to take him to and from practice, which embarrassed him to no end. The older guys were often quick with some good-natured ribbing of the younger fellas. That Exile sense of humor was evident from the very beginning, and has admittedly been a key component in their remarkable fifty-year longevity.

Mack Davenport described The Exiles from that time period as a "jukebox band." Their job was to keep up with what was hot at the time, and to play it as faithfully close to the original song as possible. They rehearsed as often as they could to sound exactly like the records. He remembered those early days of practicing in basements and playing gigs like the Richmond city park. Buzz observed that "In the beginning, every time we got noticed it was because of Jimmy Stokley. He was the primary focus. He was #1." With Stokley as their sole front man, people were definitely starting to take notice.

Stokley had an electrifying stage presence, and a gruff, gravelly, rock-n-roll voice. The guys worked hard to get their 5-part harmonies down, and they continued practicing whenever they could in Mike Howard's basement. Even way back then, vocal harmonies were an essential part of the Exile sound. J.P. still remembers their first real gig at the Richmond City Park picnic shelter. They had just started into their second song when a fist fight broke out right down in front of the stage. J.P. recalled: "We were doing all right up until that point, but the fight definitely won out for people's attention." Mike Howard also remembered one of their early gigs at a bar called the Jolly Roger in Lexington. When asked how they did, Mike replied: "Well, the crowd seemed to like us," but he admitted that the band was such a bundle of nerves that they proceeded to get extremely drunk afterwards. No matter what, The Exiles kept at it and started getting more gigs, and it wasn't long before people started paying attention to this hot new group of young long-haired guys playing all around the local music scene.

Along with a diligent rehearsal schedule, the band bettered themselves by watching other bands perform at the hottest college bar in Richmond, Specks, which was owned by Frank Nassida. Some of them weren't even old enough to get in, but they somehow managed to sneak in almost every night. There they would watch and listen and try to learn all they could about what it was to be a successful performing group. There were always one or two really hot bands, usually made up of local college kids, that would dominate the coveted weekend gigs. When The Exiles were starting out, the top group was a band called the Maroons, and after those guys graduated, Action Unlimited took over the spotlight (future friend of the band, Jerry Morse, happened to be in both of these bands; we'll see more of him later). The Exiles wanted desperately to be the next big thing at Specks, but they were still pretty green, and hadn't yet played that many shows.

Stokley, however, was a relentless promoter of the band, and he was tireless in working to get them gigs. Finally, after some serious persistence, coupled with more than a little begging and pleading, Stokley talked Frank Nassida into letting them play Specks on a slow night. Billy Luxon said that night that they were "young, hungry and dumb, and didn't have enough sense to be scared." Mike Howard also remembered those early gigs at Specks, and even though they were still learning, he said that Stokley completely captivated the audience. Mike summed it up this way: "What he [Stokley] lacked in expertise, he made up for in showmanship." Mike recalled that their performances back then were "mostly noise," and not quite up to the same standard as the more seasoned college-bar bands, but they must have shown some promise because Frank let them come back to play another night. And then another.

It wasn't long before they developed a following of their own and worked their way up to playing the big weekend nights. There was a pecking order to headlining the big weekend crowds: first, play an off-night early in the week. If that went well and they were asked back, then the band would play those nights for a while. If they were good enough they'd get moved up to bigger night, like a Thursday. The funny thing about playing weeknights was that, since it was predominantly a college crowd, the bands would all quit at 9pm. This was due solely to the fact that back then, the college girls at Eastern Kentucky University had to be in their dorms for a nine o'clock curfew. As soon as the ladies left most of the guys in the audience would follow suit, and the band would call it quits for the night. Eventually, if a band could build up a following under those conditions, they would finally be asked to play the coveted weekend spots, where there were no school curfews and everyone could stay out until closing time. And that is exactly what The Exiles did: they worked their way up from playing slow Tuesday and Wednesday nights, to the pretty good Thursday nights, to the jam-packed late-night Friday and Saturday spots. Kids from Richmond, Lexington, Bowling Green and the surrounding counties were all coming to see The Exiles play, and their popularity spread quickly by word of mouth. It was largely due to playing Specks that their stage show gained them fans all around the region.

THE EARLY YEARS

Soon The Exiles were getting gigs and playing all over central Kentucky, Southern Indiana and Ohio. J.P. Pennington observed that it probably worked in their favor that they were all from small towns - there weren't as many distractions as a big city provides, so they were able to really focus on the music. They weren't being pulled to be in other bands, which also happens in cities with a lot of competing bands and musicians. They were able to practice a lot and focus, and thus each time they played they got better and better onstage. Eventually, J.P. became lead guitarist in the band, and Paul Smith, Jr. took over on bass.

It is at this point in their history that there is another slight discrepancy about what happened next. One version goes that sometime around Christmas '65 they were playing a gig back in Richmond, and Peggy Rogers, a woman who worked for Dick Clark in Los Angeles, just happened to be home for the holidays and she caught their show. She liked what she saw, so she went back to L.A. and told Dick about them.

The other version goes that Peggy worked in Dick Clark's Cincinnati office, and as word was getting out about The Exiles regionally, she decided to drive down to check them out, and on the way down she hit a deer. It's not really clear how hitting that deer figured in to Peggy's state of mind, but however it happened, she went back and recommended The Exiles to Dick Clark, and that's all that really matters.

Back in the early 60's, there was a very popular traveling concert called the Dick Clark Caravan of Stars, which paired small, local bands with some of the top single acts/solo artists of the day, and then had national best-selling groups appear as the headliners of the show. The smaller bands would go on first to warm up the crowd with two to three songs, and then they would act as the house or back-up band for the single acts who came on next. These artists included people like Freddie Cannon ("Tallahasse Lassie," "Way Down Yonder in New Orleans"), Brian Hyland ("Itsy Bitsy Teenie Weenie Yellow Polka Dot Bikini," "Sealed With A Kiss"), Sam the Sham ("Wooly Bully," "Little Red Riding Hood"), Billy Joe Royal ("Down in the Boondocks," "I Knew You When"), Tommy Roe ("Sheila," "Dizzy"), and BJ

Thomas ("Hooked on a Feeling," "Raindrops Keep Fallin' on My Head"). After the single acts finished, the big #1 hit-recording headliners would go on. These were groups like Paul Revere and the Raiders ("Louie Louie," "Just Like Me"), Gary Lewis and the Playboys ("This Diamond Ring," "Count Me In"), the Yardbirds ("For Your Love," "Heart Full of Soul"), and the Young Rascals ("Good Lovin'," "Groovin'"). The show was a great lineup of talent of that era, and the tours were very popular.

As it so happened, The Exiles had just played a show in Lexington when they got a call from Peggy Rogers telling them to get themselves and their gear to Bowling Green's Western Kentucky University Campus, because they were to be the opening band for the Caravan of Stars tour. They had never moved so quickly in all their lives! They packed up their gear and headed out. They showed up at Diddle Arena only to receive a rather cool reception from the crowd after their first song. Undaunted, they launched into their cover of "Poor Side of Town" by Johnny Rivers. They were still quite young guys, and they were able to do the background female vocals of the song in falsetto harmony. Buzz Cornelison remembered that the audience went really quiet so that every note was heard. After they finished, the crowd erupted in applause. They loved it! That night at the end of the show the MC thanked everyone for coming and, as was customary with the Caravan of Stars tour, gave the crowd the choice to pick which act would come back out to do the encore. And that night the crowd called for The Exiles. Buzz described the event like this:

> [At first] They didn't know us and they didn't wanna see us. Yet we earned that encore from nothing. We had the Rascals on that tour and they still chose us. We really, truly earned it.

After that The Exiles were made an official offer to join the Caravan of the Stars tour. For this gig the guys would travel for 3-4 weeks at a time, with 2-3 days in between shows. They had a sleeper bus to get to the venues, which was basically a big school bus with the seats taken out in the back, and with rows of bunks installed for sleeping. They would play that day, get on the bus, and then travel for a day or two to the next show. The big headliners, of course, would get to fly rather than drive to the next venue, so early on the guys were exposed to a level of success that they wanted to achieve.

The Exiles would open up the show with a few hits of the day, songs like "Shotgun" by Junior Walker and the All Stars, and then play backup for the other acts. The Young Rascals were the headliners for most of the tours. A fellow named Jack Nance, who later co-wrote "Only Make Believe" with Conway Twitty, was their tour manager. They would finish a show and Jack would tell them to be in the parking lot at 8pm if they wanted a ride to the next one. If not, then the bus would leave without them and they'd have to find their own way to the next town (which may or may not have happened on at least one or two occasions).

Mack Davenport recounted a memorable experience when they opened a Caravan of Stars show in Cincinnati, OH. At this particular gig, The Exiles went on first as always, then Lou Christie ("Lightnin' Strikes," "Two Faces Have I"), followed by Brian Hyland, than Freddie Cannon, and then Paul Revere and The Raiders. But the surprise headliner for this particular show was the incomparable Roy Orbison and the Candymen. All the guys looked up to Roy; he was a huge star. Mack said when they were introduced to him, all they could do was stand there with their mouths open. They were absolutely speechless. Those young guys from Kentucky got to meet a living legend that day. There weren't words for Mack to to properly describe such an awesome event. Things were going well for them on the tour, and even though they were still small potatoes in the music business, they were well on their way to getting their own taste of fame.

With each performance they were learning how to be professional touring musicians, and their stage presence was getting better and better; so much so that Dick Clark himself once told Buzz Cornelison that they were probably in the top 1% of the groups playing in the US at the time. He followed up that comment by asking if Buzz knew how many bands were also in that percentile? That number was perhaps in the thousands. So what Dick Clark was really saying was that while they were good, there were thousands of other good bands out there, and the competition to get to the top of the music world would be fierce.

They had to be more than just "good" to make it. During that tour he also mentored them a bit about basic showmanship and how to be even better performers on stage. Those lessons from Dick Clark were invaluable, and the whole Caravan of Stars experience exposed them to the big time in the music business. It helped The Exiles realize that they wanted more than just to play regionally - they wanted national success. They wanted to be better than good ; they wanted to be great. They wanted to be stars.

After they had been away with the tour for a while, The Exiles came back and played their old stomping grounds at the Richmond Alumni Coliseum on Eastern Kentucky University's campus. According to J.P. Pennington, that night they were given "the longest and most honest standing ovation they've ever had." That hometown crowd was giving credit to their "locals boys done good" by giving their love and support and cheering them on all the way. This is a key part of Exile's overall success which cannot be overstated: those early Kentucky fans went with them on a journey straight to the top of the charts. The fans were an integral part of the band, and always have been, through the good times and the bad (and there were a lot of both to go around). But, at that time The Exiles were on their way up, even though soon enough there would be some changes.

In 1967, during those Caravan of Stars years, the dream to act came true for Buzz Cornelison. He landed the lead in a play, and he could no longer go on tour with the band. Fortuitously, a young man named Bernie Faulkner, from Hazard, KY, happened to have moved to Richmond to go to school at Eastern Kentucky University. One day he was out riding his motorcycle when he saw another bike parked outside of the local college bar, Specks. He used to ride with the Peacemakers back in Hazard, and he was looking for some people to ride with there in Richmond. He walked in to the bar and asked, "Whose bike is that?" As it so happened, that bike belonged to Mike Howard, who was up on the stage practicing his guitar. Bernie saw that Buzz's keyboards were there, and he asked Mike if he could play them. Mike was hesitant to let Bernie play, not only because he didn't know him, but also because Buzz was pretty protective of his keyboards. What Mike didn't know was that Bernie had a Hammond B3 at the house, and he knew his way around a keyboard. Just then, Mack Davenport came in and started playing around on the drums, and soon thereafter Paul Smith, Jr. showed up and started playing bass. They figured it would be ok if Bernie jammed with them a little bit. Billy Luxon arrived next and they were really rocking now. Finally, Buzz and Stokley showed up for what clearly was a band rehearsal, so Bernie stopped playing, jumped down from the stage, grabbed a PBR and watched them rehearse.

A few days later, Jimmy Stokley called and asked if Bernie would come back down to Specks. He asked if Bernie had ever heard of Dick Clark, and told him they were going back out with the Caravan of the Stars tour. The only problem was that Buzz had landed the lead in a play, so he wouldn't be able to go back out with them. In short, they needed a keyboard player, and they wanted Bernie to come on the tour with them. Bernie asked if he could have a couple days to think about it, so he went home to Hazard and he thought. And the more he thought about it, the more he realized that this was probably a good thing. He was in college at Eastern Kentucky University at the time, so he told his professors that he was going on tour with The Exiles and that he'd be back to in time to take the mid-terms. He never failed, he said, but he definitely had to drop some classes, and he may have gotten a few C's along the way.

On the first day of the new tour they went to Charlotte, NC. It was a scramble because in just one day, Bernie and the guys had to learn five different artists' songs to play as their back-up band. Most of the guys were self-taught and couldn't read music to save their souls, so the music charts meant nothing. Bernie said that night they managed to fake it, and people seemed to like it, so things were alright. On that particular tour, Paul Revere and the Raiders needed horns for some of their songs, and they asked if any members of The Exiles could play. Billy Luxon had his trumpet, and it turned out that Bernie happened to play sax as well as keyboards, so he and Billy got to play with Paul Revere and the Raiders as well as The Exiles on that leg of the tour. It was a great opportunity, and they had a really good time getting to know the Raiders. Bernie said it was all like a dream come true.

By now they had a few of the Caravan of Stars tours under their belt, so they packed up their equipment in a Chevy Corvair van and went to where all the good bands go to make it - New York City. On the drive up they had two cars - Mike Howard was driving the van with all their equipment with Mack Davenport riding shotgun, and they were following another car with the rest of the guys. Mike couldn't remember who exactly was driving the other car. It is important to remember that in those pre-cell phone days there often wasn't good communication between drivers. If someone had to make a rest stop, or one of the cars needed gas, you had better be paying attention when they headed for that next exit. Well, on the way up things were going just fine, when all of a sudden and without warning, the driver of the other car, which was in front of Mike, quickly turned off onto an exit ramp to get to a gas station. Mike had to throw on the brakes and swerve to make the turn in time to take the exit. Mike figured they might as well get some gas, too, so he pulled up to the gas station and waited for an attendant to fill up the tank (no cell phones AND no self-serve? It's almost inconceivable today).

At about that time a man walked up to the driver's side of the car, and without even looking Mike told him to fill 'er up and to please check the oil. Mike happened to be looking over at Mack, whose eyes had gone as wide as saucers. Well, that man turned out to be a state trooper who had seen The Corvair brake hard and swerve off the interstate, so he had followed to check them out. The officer thought Mike was being a smart ass with his request, so he issued a ticket for them to appear before a judge right then and there. They had to go to night court and wake a judge, who was none too happy to be awaked to see such a disreputable group of long-haired Southern boys. He made them pay a $60 fine, which was quite hefty at the time, and they were finally back on their way. It was not the most auspicious start to their trip toward the big city, but nevertheless, it didn't deter them from their mission. They made it up to New York City all in one piece, and none the worse for the wear, albeit a few dollars poorer than when they started out.

Perhaps it goes without saying that the big city was different from anything these country boys had ever experienced. They had never seen anything quite like it. They rode the subway for the first time, and saw myriad things they had never seen back home in Kentucky. Bernie Faulkner, ever the student, somehow managed to even take some classes while they were there. Every once in a while they would get some flack about being "Kentucky rednecks," but they tried not to let it bother them too much. They were a polite, educated group of young men (some might even say "Southern gentlemen"), and they knew better than to let things like that get to them. As is often the case, actions speak louder than words, and they knew they were professional musicians and that their playing would speak for itself.

They ended up staying for a while at the Broadway Central Hotel in the East Village, a once glorious luxury hotel that had become dilapidated over time and eventually turned into a pretty shady establishment (In fact, a few years later in 1973, a wall of the hotel actually collapsed, killing several residents). Next, they sub-let an apartment way uptown on 96th Street and West End Avenue. That apartment was so disgusting that when thy left they didn't feel too badly about further trashing the place. During that time they had a gig playing 7 nights/week, 6 sets/night from 9pm until 3am at a rough bar called Cholly's, up in the Bronx. After that gig ended they went and stayed in a motel in Queens, where they played the Hockomock Club. One night while they were playing someone broke into their van and stole some of their equipment. Those were hard times, not very glamorous at all, but they still managed to have some fun. Billy Luxon summed up the New York days like this:

> We were six young, inexperienced, immature guys, and we were up there existing and surviving by ourselves. Not that we had a lot of money, but we got everything done we wanted to, had a great time, and met a lot of people. It was all good.

Not all their gigs in New York were terrible, and many were definitely interesting. Mack Davenport recalled one night where they played a private black-tie event at The Scene East, the basement bar of the Delmont Hotel, on Park Avenue. At this particular event The Exiles opened up for Tiny Tim, of "Tiptoe Through the Tulips" fame. They went on first and everything went well; the crowd really seemed to like them. Then Tiny Tim went on and something crazy happened: the mood in the room changed, and the guests turned on Tiny Tim. Mack said it was like a scene from a movie - people actually started throwing chairs and turning over tables. It was total mayhem. The Exiles were just glad that it wasn't their fault that the crowd revolted, and they got the heck out of dodge. They would never forget seeing all those high-class New York Park Avenue folks in tuxedoes losing their minds like that. And here people thought that *they* were the rednecks. That night they learned that people from all walks of life misbehave, from time to time.

They were playing gigs all over New York, desperately trying to get a big record deal. Along the way they ended up meeting some interesting New York characters, like a guy named Phillip Basile, a club owner and band manager who reputedly had ties to the Lucchese crime family. Phil saw them at a gig and said was interested in having them play his clubs, but supposedly he had just one question for them: "Why should I hire you? I have a jukebox that plays the same things you do." That's when they realized that they could be the best cover band in the world, but they needed to do something to make themselves stand out, to be original. They started sitting in their hotel room and taking current hits and old standards and changing them up. The singers would work up the vocals first, and then the instruments would follow. Even though they were performing cover songs, they soon found ways to re-arrange the songs and give them their own, distinct sound. In this way they began to really stand out from the other bands on the circuit.

Another way The Exiles stood out was they played LOUDLY. Like really, really loud. Bernie Faulkner's uncle was a doctor, who at one point gave Bernie an expensive pair of custom earplugs to wear while he was playing, in order to save his hearing. But Bernie said, "Playing with earplugs was like taking a shower with a raincoat on." He just couldn't play like that, and his bandmates (and many fellow musicians outside the band) felt the same at the time. It wasn't until much later that many would realize the permanent damage, like loss of hearing and tinnitus that accompanies playing and seeing loud live music on a regular basis. It's pretty safe to say, however, that even if they had known the full extent of the dangers to their hearing, it still wouldn't have made a slight bit of difference. That's just rock-n-roll.

But back to the story at hand: Phil ended up hiring them to play a show on Long Island at his bar, the Action House, with a band called the Vanilla Fudge, who ironically became famous for performing covers of The Supremes' "You Keep Me Hangin' On," and the Beatles' "Ticket To Ride." Bernie remembered watching the Vanilla Fudge keyboard player and being blown away by how good that guy was. They also played some shows at that venue with The Vagrants, a Long Island band that ended up having a national hit with the song "Oh Those Eyes." Again, it was early experiences like these that helped the guys get better at their own live shows. They may have been top dogs in Richmond, KY, but on tour in major cities they were up against the best, and that only made them step up their game. They continued to observe other bands carefully, and incorporate some of their ideas and make them their own. And now the way The Exiles would re-arrange a song and make it new and different became part of their trademark sound, and it was a great way to be original in a time when club bands were only performing covers.

In 1968, The Exiles came back to Kentucky and did a show at Club 68 in Lebanon, and a band called Raintree was their opening act. Greg Martin, a local musician and future member of The Kentucky Headhunters, was in that band. This is how he remembered that show:

> We [Raintree] had a chance to open up for Exile at Club 68. Now, oddly enough, I had never seen the band live. I'd heard their records, but I worked all the time and just never had seen them. So anyway, we got down and did our meager opening set, and Exile comes out and blows the roof off the place. And it scared me to death. I went, OK, if I'm going to do this, eitherI 'm going to get serious about it or I'm just gonna play weekends. I was really in awe of the guitarist, J.P. Pennington, and I

think it pushed me. That was a deciding moment.

Greg went on to add that "They are the finest band to come out of Kentucky."

Fellow Kentucky Headhunter, Fred Young, also spoke of just how influential The Exiles were on the local music scene:

> We learned so much from just seeing those guys. Not only just listening to them play, but their style. They were special people, and great players... They're our heroes. They always will be. They're the guys we grew up listening to.

So many local and regional musicians looked up to them. The Exiles were the cream of the crop, and it just didn't get any better.

Fred's brother, Richard Young, who is also in the Kentucky Headhunters, added:

I remember thinking to myself, the first time I saw them play, if you guys look like this and act like this, you guys are gonna get there. Exile had a vibe. They were different. Not metal, not light rock, they just did this Kentucky rock-n-roll thing. In Kentucky we have this mindset in folks out there that it couldn't be rock-n-roll, because it's from Kentucky. It's actually quite fragile and it can be damaging.

Richard so eloquently summed up what it was like for them to be rock-n-roll musicians from Kentucky, struggling to convince the world that they were good enough to play on the national stage. As many Kentuckians can attest, there is a certain image of the "Kentucky redneck" that not only still exists, but is continually perpetuated throughout the media. It was even worse back when the guys were trying to make it big in the 60s and 70s, and even into the 80s. I distinctly remember once, on a trip to L.A., being asked if we had electricity and wore shoes back home. A Southern accent is derided in other states, and often equated with lack of intelligence or eloquence. It can be a frustrating stereotype to overcome, but a healthy sense of humor goes a long way, and The Exiles always maintained a positive attitude and a professional demeanor when dealing with those who would try to bring them down. Fortunately, there were supporters like Greg Martin, Richard and Fred Young, and their growing fan base to encourage them along the way.

An interesting fact about The Exiles is that from very early on, and all throughout the years, they have operated as a democracy before making major decisions that concern everyone in the band. Whenever a big decision is to be made, they hold a meeting and make that decision democratically, with the majority winning the vote. In 1969, it became necessary to hold one of their special band meetings, because Buzz Cornelison had finished his role in the play and wanted to come back to the band. Buzz was an original member of The Exiles, so when he wanted to come back, of course they gave him preference. What they needed to do, however, was make a decision about what to do with Bernie Faulkner. After they had met for a while, they called Bernie in and gave him their decision: they would have two keyboard players. Buzz would play classic piano on his keyboards, while Bernie would play rock-n-roll keyboard. The Hammond B3 that Bernie played had a distinctive sound that enhanced background vocals, which resulted in an effect that was almost like doubling their vocals, and they really liked it. With the decision to use both guys, their sound was richer than ever.

The 70s were fast approaching, and the times, as they say, they were a-changing. Paul Smith, Jr was drafted and went off to Vietnam in either '67 or '68. He did not return to the band after he completed his tour of duty. In February 1969, Mike Howard, too, was drafted and went off to Vietnam. Of his time with the band Mike said, "We didn't make a lot of money, but we survived and had big fun." But it turns out that these weren't the only changes that would happen to The Exiles: soon thereafter, J.P. decided that he wanted to go back to college to play basketball, so he temporarily left the band. They had a guy named Larry Davis play guitar with them for a while, but Larry didn't work out, so they asked J.P. to come back. Even with these shake-ups, they always knew what they wanted - their chance at the big time. But they needed a major label record deal to make that happen.

In the mid- to late 60s, The Exiles finally decided to start writing and performing their own original music. Stokley and J.P. wrote their first song together, "John Weatherman," and they wanted to get it recorded on a major label. Up until this point, The Exiles had recorded a couple of minor local hits on small record labels, such as Wooden Nickel and later Date Records, which was a branch of Columbia. The song "Mary on the Beach" was recorded around 1967 on Date Records. "Thunder in Eden" was recorded at a studio on Broadway in New York, the same studio where the Tokens recorded "The Lion Sleeps Tonight." Slowly but surely, people were catching on to the original songs and they were touring more than ever. The home-town crowds loved the new songs, and they became local hits.

The Exiles got a big gig opening for Tommy James ("Mony Mony," "Crimson and Clover") in Baton Rouge, LA. J.P. recalled Tommy coming up to them after show. He said he liked what he saw, and that he had been writing songs in the hopes of having other artists record them. He had one song in particular in mind that he had written that he thought would work well for them. Tommy then sent The Exiles the demo for a song called "Church Street Soul Revival." J.P. and the rest of the band were blown away. It was great, and now they had their very own song written by Tommy James! It would be a sure-fire hit. Tommy got them studio time, and back to New York City they went. They drove the 16 hours straight up to record their new song.

Due to their association with Tommy James, their label decided to move The Exiles from their smaller subsidiary, Date, up to Columbia Records. They had finally achieved their goal - they had a record deal with a major label! They were so excited, they wanted to record the track and get it right out to Columbia for distribution. When they arrived in Manhattan, they went immediately into the studio. Tommy James surprised them by sitting in on the session and even playing guitar with them on the track. After "Church Street" was finished, they also went on to record "John Weatherman," that very first song written by J.P. and Stokley together, as the b-side for the record. It was a truly monumental moment for the band. In all, they drove up 16 hours, were in the studio for about 24 hours straight, and nonetheless they decided to drive straight back to Kentucky that very next night. J.P. said that they were so tired they had to take turns taking 20 minute shifts behind the wheel just to make it back home alive. But make it they did, back home to Kentucky, where they were already becoming stars.

It now becomes necessary to veer away from The Exiles' story as a band to explain a bit about the music business and radio in the late 60s and early 70s. It's a bit pedantic but also very important, so here goes: in the 50s, 60s and 70s, people listened to music primarily over AM radio. The problem with AM radio, though, is that it has a lot of limitations. It doesn't reach as far as say, FM radio, and the radio waves are easily disrupted by buildings, weather, and even certain lighting. For example, an AM station will go out while you drive through a tunnel. The waves can't penetrate the structure, so all you hear is fuzz until you reach the other side. The main result of the limitations of AM radio was that many different small, local stations cropped up all across America, all of them broadcasting different content. Sure, there was Dick Clark and the Billboard Top 100 (which became the Hot 100 in

1958) keeping track of what was popular nationally, but regionally and locally it was relatively easy to get local stations to also play songs by local artists. So back then there were hits by local bands at local stations, because the DJs would like a certain song and play it often, putting it into heavy rotation, and people could request to hear the song, just as would happen nationally, but on a much, much smaller scale.

It is in this way that The Exiles got a lot of airplay in smaller markets, and rose to the top of various local charts, but ultimately found national fame elusive. "Church Street" ended up being a #1 record in many different, smaller markets. It went to #1 or at least the top 5 all over Kentucky, Ohio, Indiana, and then in many towns across the U.S. as well. In those pre-internet days, music spread slowly from town to town, market to market. Seeing how college kids were a big demographic for The Exiles, kids would come home from being away at school and go out at night and hear them play, and they would like the music so they would buy the single. Then they would take that record to their college town and play it at parties, and ask the local DJs to play it at that local radio station. The song would almost invariably become a hit, so The Exiles would get booked to go and play that town, and thus their popularity spread and grew. But all of this would happen in fits and spurts, and "Church Street" just never caught on nationwide all at the same time. The song ended up charting in Billboard at just over 100, in the what was known as the "Bubbling Under" section of the Hot 100. The Exiles previously had other local and regional hits with their songs "Mary on the Beach" and "Thunder in Eden," but they just couldn't seem to crack into the Top 100. At least, not until that one song, but that's coming up soon enough.

Now some might ask why, with their early access to and affiliation with Dick Clark, they couldn't get on American Bandstand, which surely would have helped to shoot them to the top of the charts? Well, back in 1960 there was something called the Payola scandal, which basically charged that radio DJs were taking cash, or "payola," from the record companies who represented certain artists to play only those songs by those artists and put them into heavy rotation, therefore practically ensuring that those songs became hits. It was such a big deal that Congress convened an official inquiry, and Dick

Clark himself was asked to testify, due to his multi-tiered involvement in the record industry, and his extensive influence as a musical taste-maker. He came out largely unscathed, but one of the consequences was that he couldn't have groups with whom he had had previous affiliations on the show unless they already had Top 100 hits.

What that meant for The Exiles was that they couldn't go onto American Bandstand, a hit show that probably would have garnered them the national recognition they so desired, until they already had a top 100 hit. It was kind of a rock-n-roll Catch-22. In later years Dick Clark wanted to sign them to a record label he was starting, but due to the repercussions of the byzantine rules and regulations that went into effect after the Payola scandal, he could not. But he did record a very lovely endorsement of them on cassette tape that they could take with them to music studios when they were trying to get a deal. Dick Clark was very good to them, and will be forever remembered fondly for all he contributed not only to Exile, but to music in America as a whole. The Exiles would just have to find another way to make it to the top.

THE 70s

As has been observed many times before, the decade from the 60s to the 70s saw many changes in the world politically, socially, and musically, and The Exiles were changing right along with the times. Even though they were doing great at home and regionally, they kept touring and reaching for that elusive national fame that seemed just outside of their grasp. But after a while, the enthusiasm both within and outside the band started to lose some steam. They were very disappointed that "Church Street" didn't propel them into the Top 100, and that they had thus far been unable to reach the level of stardom that they truly desired.

Due to these circumstances, and factoring in a string of bad contracts and record deals, several members decided it was time to leave the band. J.P. Pennington left them for a second time to go to Laguna Beach, CA with one of his cousins, so they could make a go of shopping some songs they had written together to record companies and other artists out there. Mack Davenport, too, decided it was time to go. He was burned out, and it just wasn't fun anymore. He said they had had a good record with "Church Street," but when they came back to town after touring and trying to make that song a national hit, there just wasn't much going on. In the end Mack described the whole experience thusly:

> It was a learning experience. It was fun; it was a job; it was a chore. But it was very enlightening, very educational. I got to go to a lot of places I wouldn't have been able to go, got to meet a lot of people, see a lot of things. Some of the things I probably shouldn't have seen, but it was quite an experience. I wouldn't have traded it for the world. I probably would have been better off if I'd done something else, but I wouldn't have enjoyed it nearly as much.

At this point, the remaining guys were lower than they had ever been. They even came close to giving up completely on the band, but Stokley somehow managed to convince them to give it one last chance. They still had gigs on the books, so they scrambled to quickly replace J.P. and

Mack for the upcoming shows. Bobby Johns, whom the guys nicknamed "Lightning" for his inability to hurry up while they were on tour, was hired to play drums. Bobby brought along his friend and former band mate, Kenny Weir, to play guitar. Bill Kennon was then hired to play bass. Kenny and Bobby were more into hard rock than R&B, and with their addition to The Exiles, the band's sound definitely started to change. Billy Luxon heard the direction their sound was going, and thought to himself, "There are no horns in hard rock," so he left the band as well. He ended up opening his own very successful Richmond college-band bar, J Sutter's Mill.

Bobby Johns and Kenny Weir had just two days to learn all the songs, and on that second night they played the Stake Out in Richmond, KY. Bobby said there was a lot of pressure on them, because The Exiles had such a great reputation for being a really good live band, but their first show together went really well nonetheless. Even with all these shake-ups The Exiles managed to continue playing, and they were still great live. J.P. ended up coming back to Kentucky after a few months in California, and he soon re-joined the band. Kenny went from guitar to bass, with

J.P. now playing lead guitar. This new lineup showed a lot of promise, and all was well again for the guys. People responded well to the new musical direction they were taking.

Around 1973 The Exiles became known simply as Exile. They recorded their first Exile album on Wooden Nickel records, which was next door to the Gaslight Club in Chicago. Wooden Nickel had a distribution deal with RCA Records, and was most famous at the time for recording the rock band Styx. They followed up "Church Street" with a funky song called "Devil's Bite," which was written by Todd Rundgren ("Hello It's Me," "Bang the Drum All Day"). Exile's producer at the time, Bill Traut, knew Rundgren, who was an accomplished engineer, producer and musician. Traut got "Devil's Bite" from Rundgren, and Exile recorded it up at Paragon Studios in Chicago.

They needed a cover for the album, so RCA set up a photo shoot in New York with famous rock-n-roll photographer Ace Lehman, who had also done an album cover for Elvis Presley. They were really excited, and in typical Exile fashion they drove the van straight up from Richmond, KY to New York City, where they immediately went to the photo shoot. They later found out that one of the ways RCA decided to promote the band was by submitting photos from that shoot to a girly magazine called Genesis, where they were featured in an edgy article entitled "Exile is a Stone Bitch!" While J.P. was proudly showing the article to his dad, the magazine fell open to the centerfold. His dad looked at him and cracked "Is that you?" It's a good thing his dad had a sense of humor! Rock-n-roll in the 70s was not for the faint at heart.

After they finished up with the photo shoot with Ace it was well past midnight, and they were completely exhausted. This time their label had gotten some rooms for them, so they headed over to the hotel only to find that, due to the late hour, their rooms had already been given away. They desperately wanted to get some rest, so rather than drive the sixteen hours straight back to Richmond like they always did, they instead tried heading back down the highway a bit to see if they could find a place with some vacancy. The ended up finding a truck stop that had some rooms available. They were so relieved! But when they got to their rooms there was one small problem: at this fine establishment each of the rooms had at least one of the windows broken out, and it was winter, and it was snowing. Snow was actually blowing into the rooms while they tried to rest up and shower. They ended up getting about two hours of sleep before they gave up and drove all the way back home. It seems they just weren't meant to get much rest on those long trips to and from New York City.

Soon they went on tour to support the new Exile album. They got a gig opening for The Stories ("Brother Louie") at the famous Whisky A Go-Go in Los Angeles, and on that trip they stayed in L.A. for about a week. While there they also played the Starwood, another famous club. Outside the Starwood was a huge billboard, and painted on it was their album cover that Ace Lehman had shot, larger-than-life, and in great detail. They had really hit the big time now! They met and hung out with Jeff Fenholt, the actor who played Jesus in Andrew Lloyd Webber's outrageous and shocking new rock opera, Jesus Christ Superstar. Possibly due to this experience Exile decided to add a cover of the song "Jesus is Just Alright" to their repertoire. They first performed that song at one of their shows in California, and the crowd loved it.

Yet even with the new album, and appearing on billboards, and hobnobbing with Broadway actors, they still had to drive to their own gigs, no matter how far away, in their old GMC van. Bobby Johns remembered how in those days, they would pack all their equipment and themselves into the van and drive from coast to coast. The only way they could sleep was to take turns lying side-by-side, sometimes three at a time, flat underneath the seats. As far as touring went, they hadn't come much further than the old Caravan of Stars bus. It was not a comfortable ride, but it worked. They always got where they needed to go.

Around this time, future friend of the band and Kentucky Headhunter, Richard Young, remembered seeing Exile play the Greensburg, KY Park. It had an open-air auditorium, and the place was jam-packed. He said Exile came on and blew the crowd away. Their music, the stage show, everything was completely over-the-top. Richard said he thought to himself, as a young musician, "You gotta be this good or don't do it." No other band in the region looked or played like them. Exile was an inspiration to all the up-and-coming musicians in the area. They were true rock-n-roll stars up there on that stage.

After the show, Richard and his friends went to get some food and hang out at The Green Jersey, a little root beer stand near the park. As he was sitting there, the Exile van pulled up and Stokley got out and walked up to the window to order a burger. Richard and his friends were in awe to see him offstage. The young girl at the counter told Stokley, "I'm sorry, we just closed for the night." Upon hearing this he just smiled and said, "That's ok, baby. We'll just go on down the road." No ego; no tantrum; no "do-you-know-who-I-am?" screaming fit. Stokley just sauntered back to the van and away they went, just like that. Richard said "It was that simple, because they were gentlemen." Richard remembered that moment many times in his career with the Headhunters. He realized, "Once the lights go out, you're just a dude. Rock stars get turned down, too." It was important to stay grounded, to hear "no" every once in a while, and to stay humble. It was a valuable life lesson to learn as a young musician, or any profession for that matter. Moreover, it is also a reflection on the kind, sweet nature of Jimmy Stokley, who could rock so hard on stage, yet be so gentle in real life.

The guys in Exile learned many life lessons from that time period as well. No matter the obstacles or how hard they had to work, they kept right on at it. They knew something big was just around the next corner. Even though "Devil's Bite" was a great song, they had the exact same problem with it as they had with "Church Street." It became a hit in many small local markets, but it just couldn't seem to catch national attention, and it didn't crack the Billboard Top 100.

Yet at the same time, locally, Exile was getting bigger and bigger. Doug Breeding, friend of the band, musician and club-owner, remembered going to see them in the early 70s with future band members Marlon Hargis and Sonny LeMaire, who just happened to be seeing them for the very first time. Exile was opening a department store called McAlpin's in the Lexington Mall on Richmond Road. Stokley strutted out on stage with his long hair, spandex pants and knee-high boots and cautioned everyone in front of the speakers to step back, because it was about to get loud. They then proceeded to rock that crowds' socks off. They had successfully moved from being an R&B cover band to a full-fledged rock band, and their fans absolutely ate it up. They loved that rock-n-roll Exile sound.

Doug said that Exile put on such a great live show and had such good musicians that everyone in Central Kentucky and the region looked up to them:

> It's hard to explain just how big they were to other musicians... I have never heard anybody who was better at walking on stage, plugging in and playing, no matter who was in the lineup. They were just the tops... They sounded so good and had great singers, great players - always.

He also said Exile cultivated a certain mystery around themselves. They had such a good reputation that they were basically able to pick and choose where they played, and they would only play one night at a venue instead of booking multiple nights in a row at the same place, which was customary. That exclusivity would create demand, and made their shows all the more special. As has been mentioned before, Stokley was such an outstanding presence on stage that they were often known unofficially as "Jimmy Stokley and Exile." Friend of the band Richard Young, from the Kentucky Headhunters, remembered Stokley in those days. He said:

> There are very few dynamic front men. I can name them on one hand: Mick Jagger, Robert Plant in his heyday, and Jimmy Stokley. He was a cross between Mick Jagger and Todd Rundgren. He had this look. He was so unusual: he had the lips of Jagger and the hair of Rundgren.

In retrospect, Jimmy Stokley was way ahead of his time. He was truly something to behold when he got up on that stage.

So things were going great for them locally, but still more changes were to come. As it turns out, the next change to the band involved Bernie

Faulkner. His father, who owned a 3rd generation car dealership, had become ill. They were playing back up in New York with Woodstock performer Richie Havens ("Freedom," "Here Comes the Sun"), when Bernie informed them that he had to leave the band to tend to family matters. The band had gotten used to the dual keyboard sound Buzz and Bernie had going, however, and they wanted to keep that sound intact. So, when Bernie left they decided to hire another keyboard player. Marlon Hargis came into the band in 1974.

Marlon grew up in Somerset, KY and started playing music around town in '62. He had actually seen one of the Dick Clark Caravan of Stars tours when it was in Lexington at the old football stadium. He couldn't recall if The Exiles where on that tour in particular, but he did remember that the Knickerbockers ("Lies," "One Track Mind"), and the Young Rascals were the headliners. As a young musician he had of course heard of The Exiles, but he hadn't yet met any of them. Some years later he went to see them play a dance at the community college there in Somerset, and he remembers them being very cool. They definitely lived up to the hype.

Marlon went on to join Gary and Sherry Edwards, a successful band from the the Louisville area, and it was around that time that he met J.P. Pennington and Kenny Weir. After leaving Gary and Sherry Edwards, Marlon moved to Lexington and got hired to manage a popular local recording studio, Lemco Studios, which was owned by sound engineer and friend of the band, Cecil Jones, who has since passed away. Cecil used to hire J.P. and Kenny to do session work at Lemco, and it was there that Marlon first met them and got to know them better. At night, Marlon played with friend of the band and club owner, Doug Breeding, and future band member Sonny LeMaire, in a band called Powder Keg. Due to his association with both Lemco and Doug, when it came time to hire another keyboard player, Marlon was the band's first choice.

Therefore, when Bernie left in 1974, J.P. called up Marlon and asked him to join the band. After just one or two rehearsals, Marlon played his fist gig with Exile at The Family Dog, a well-known Eastern Kentucky University bar. Initially he was really nervous, not just to be the newest member of a successful local rock band, but also because he was a little worried that Stokley would have an arrogant, rock-star attitude. Marlon was pleasantly surprised to find that, while he did have that larger-than-life rock-star persona onstage, Stokley was one of the sweetest, nicest guys Marlon had ever met. Stokley wasn't egotistical at all; he was just a really genuine, good guy. In fact, Marlon thought all the members of Exile were great guys, and they got along really well. They were all hopeful that the changes happening in the band would yield positive results. After each tour they were welcomed back to Kentucky as full-fledged rock stars, and they always had packed crowds for their shows.

During this new round of changes to the band, the next member to join Exile was Danny Williams, also in '74, to replace Kenny Weir on bass. As was the case with many of the other band members, Danny had also seen Exile perform around the area before he was ever asked to join the band. For Danny, he had seen them play at Specks back in '68 or '69, and he was very impressed. Danny later played in a band called Hickory Smoke with none other than Marlon Hargis. Five or six years after that, Marlon called Danny up to ask him to sit in on some jam sessions with Exile at Lemco Studios. They liked what they heard, and a day or two later they invited Danny to join the band. Danny was already in a group called the Berkshire 7 when he was asked to join, but he knew that Exile was the band that everyone looked up to in the region, so he decided to quit that band and give it a go with Exile.

To quickly get him up to speed, J.P. gave Danny some tapes of their songs so he could learn the bass parts. Danny gave them a listen but then had to tell him "I'm sorry, but I don't play like that." J.P. and the guys were a bit panicked when they heard that, but Danny explained that Kenny Weir and he had vastly different playing styles: Danny had a simple, solid, straight-to-the-point style. He often played right along with the drum beat. Kenny, on the other hand, did not. Danny went ahead and learned the songs, but he changed the bass line to fit his own style of playing. He remembered being terrified to play his first gig together with Exile and to see how they would react to his different approach to the songs. For that first show they played a small concert hall in Indiana with another 70s band called Limousine, and it went really well. So well, in fact, that Stokley turned around and told Danny "I didn't know we could be that good." Danny was overjoyed that they liked and appreciated his new style. With the addition of each new member their sound was evolving.

Exile had gotten so good and was so well-known, that in either late '75 or early '76 they got a huge gig opening for Fleetwood Mac, who had just released their eponymous album containing the hits "Rhiannon," "Over My Head," and "Say You Love Me." Unfortunately, this was one of the rare few instances in which Exile did not have a good rapport with the other band they were working with. To make matters worse, at one of the venues in Indianapolis, Indiana, both bands had to share a single dressing room. Even though they were all jammed together in rather cramped quarters, none of the members of Fleetwood Mac would look at the guys in Exile, much less speak to them. Fleetwood Mac totally and completely ignored them. Danny remembered a moment when Mick Fleetwood and he were both using the only large mirror in the room to get ready for the show. Danny said that Mick just stared straight ahead at himself, refusing to even catch Danny's eye. This was, by far, one of the few times when there wasn't an ounce of band camaraderie between Exile and the other band. That just wasn't how the guys in Exile operated, nor the other acts with whom they worked.

Rest assured that Exile didn't let that experience get them down. Rather, Bobby Johns said that they were instead completely focused on making the band bigger and better.

He described them thusly:

> We were pretty OCD. We were obsessed with it 24/7. We didn't do anything but Exile. That's all there was. It was total commitment all the time... We wanted to be something different. We treated it as something special, and it was.

They re-invested all the money they made playing shows back into the band: the light show, sound system, stage outfits, advertising. They were their own guerrilla marketers. According to Booby they made Exile stickers and put them "everywhere that would stick." They even traded in the old GMC van that had served them so well and bought a brand new Winnebago so they could travel in more comfort. But with all that money going back into the band, they also managed to hold down their income to almost nothing. As a result, they sometimes would get two bedroom apartments and live together as roommates to keep expenses down. They were living and breathing Exile 24/7.

Next, they decided to have an even more dramatic stage presence by giving their look an overhaul. They came up with a new rule for their on-stage appearance: If you could wear it on the street, then you couldn't wear it on stage. They worked with a costume designer named Carolyn McWharter, who owned a shop called Tiger Rags in Daytona Beach, FL. She designed several of their stage costumes from that era. And finally, they came up with the idea that, at the end of each and every show, they would leave the stage and then come back out for the encore dressed all in white and shining sequins. It must have been a sight to see. Visually and musically, they were embracing a flashy 70s rock-n-roll persona and making everyone around them sit up and take notice.

On their various tours, the guys had become friends with Bud Asher, who owned the Safari Motel in Daytona Beach, FL, where they had a standing gig to play every Spring Break (which is where they met costume designer Carolyn McWhorter). Dane Eric was a successful rock-n-roll radio DJ in Florida who was a big supporter of the band in those early days. Dane ended up moving to Ohio to become Program Director for TV station WMFJ. But back then, Dane was an early fan and unofficial promoter of the band, and he eventually became their manager. He knew legendary Australian producer/songwriter Mike Chapman, and Dane sent cassette tapes of the band to him in the hopes of getting Chapman interested in the great band he was managing, Exile. He succeeded in persuading Chapman to fly in from L.A. to see them play the grand opening of Kirklevington Apartments in Lexington, KY, and he liked what he saw. At the time, Chapman was actively searching for bands who were on the cusp of making it big, and he thought

Exile had exactly what it took to be the next big thing in music.

As a bit of background, Mike Chapman and his partner Nicky Chinn (known collectively as writer/producer duo Chinnichap) were huge in the 70s European glam rock music scene, and they had written hits for artists like The Sweet ("The Ballroom Blitz") and Suzi Quatro ("Can the Can"). They had also produced Nick Gilders' album *City Nights*, which contained the breakout hit "Hot Child in the City." In 1977, the duo took Exile down to Nashville and got them a song deal with Atco, a subsidiary of Atlantic Records. Their next order of business was to cut a single produced and written by Chinnichap, called "Try It On." It reached #97 on the Billboard charts. Finally! They had cracked the Hot 100. They hoped and wondered if maybe this time they would go all the way to the top of the charts. Things were moving fast for Exile, and they held on tight and prepared for the best.

"Try It On" definitely reflected the disco sound that was consuming the radio airwaves at the time. According to Billboard's Top 100 from the year

1977, a majority of the top hits that year were disco songs: Andy Gibb's "I Just Want To Be Your Everything," Emotions' "Best of My Love," K.C. And the Sunshine Band's "I'm your Boogie Man," and Abba's "Dancing Queen" were some of the top-selling songs that year. Even though they still considered themselves very much a rock-n-roll band, under Chapman's direction they definitely co-opted a more pop/disco sound. Their next single would continue in that direction and propel them straight to super-stardom, but in the meantime their music careers pretty much stalled. They believed if the single "Try It On" did well then they could go on to record a whole album with Atlantic and become big, big stars. But "Try It On" failed to impress. It peaked at #97 on the Billboard charts and then just disappeared. Atlantic didn't end up offering them an album deal. The guys were convinced that this was their only shot to work with the great Mike Chapman, and they had blown it. Once again, they had a great song that just couldn't quite catch national attention. It was a blow to all their hard work and determination, and it ate away at their optimism. Exile experienced yet another personnel change-up.

In June of 1977, Steve Goetzman joined the band to replace Bobby Johns on drums. Steve was 12 or 13 years old when "Church Street" was a regional hit on the radio, and he remembered the song well. Years later, Steve ended up working as a session musician for Lemco Studios. Cecil Jones was then using Steve and Exile band members J.P. Pennington, Marlon Hargis and Danny Williams as house rhythm section for jingles and ads recorded at his studio. Coincidentally, Steve and J.P. were roommates at the time in a two bedroom apartment. Since several of them had already worked with Steve at the studio, and they were familiar with his style and personality, they thought that he was not only the logical but the best choice for the job. Steve said he was really enjoying doing studio session work, so he asked for a weekend to think about the offer to join the band. He liked the flexibility of getting to play with a variety of talented local musicians versus being stuck with the same group of guys in a band day in and day out. But of course, that next week he went ahead and accepted the offer to join the band.

As seemed to be the case with all the new additions to Exile, they only rehearsed one or two times before Steve played his first gig with them at The Camelot in Lexington, KY. He said the show was a bit rough for him because he didn't feel like he was ready to play out with them yet. He was used to rehearsing 2-3 hours a day, 4 or 5 times a week, and he was a bit shocked to learn that by this point Exile actually practiced very little. He'd ask "Guys, don't you wanna rehearse?" And they'd say, "Sure! What song do you wanna work on?" They didn't rehearse very much by then, and Steve says they don't practice together much to this day. Despite this fact, it is evident that they have a way of gelling when they all get together onstage. Marlon Hargis described what they have as "musical magic." Steve quickly became a part of the magic that makes Exile click.

The next new hire for the band was bass player (and my father) Sonny LeMaire. Sonny arrived in Lexington, KY from the Southern Indiana/ Northern Kentucky music scene in 1970, and he was already quite familiar with many of the musicians in Lexington from playing around the clubs and bars regionally. Like many before him, Sonny also remembered going to see the Caravan of Stars tour one year when it was in

Louisville, KY. He knew that the hot band in the area was Exile, and within the first few years of moving to Lexington, Sonny met and worked with several of the current and future band members in various bands and projects.

For example, it is believed that Sonny first met Marlon Hargis sometime in 1970 at a Lexington bar called La Flame on Winchester Road. La Flame was actually a supper club, which meant that it served a full food menu while also featuring live entertainment up on a stage called the bandstand. Jerry Morse, local musician, restaurateur, and friend of the band, owned La Flame at the time. He made the place famous with his wild idea to have an after-hours breakfast buffet, so that all the local musicians and club-goers could eat after a long night of performing and partying. In the 1970s, Lexington's laws required bars to stop serving liquor at 1 AM, and live music had to halt at that time as well. Jerry thought it would be great to get a portable breakfast buffet cart and wheel it out onto the dance floor after the bars officially closed so that local musicians could have a place to eat and relax after their gigs. Jerry recounted that many of these local musicians were working steadily, 5 or 6 nights a week, so they rarely got a chance to see each other perform. He decided that the "fee" for the breakfast for the musicians would be that they would all have to get up and jam acoustically in a session on the bandstand. It was a wild success, and the buffet/bandstand drew people from all over the region, including Sonny and Marlon. As mentioned previously, Sonny and Marlon ended up playing together with Doug Breeding in the band Powder Keg at The Terrace Room in the Eastland Bowling Lanes. When Marlon left to join Exile, Sonny continued to play with Doug. They had a steady gig and good crowds, and Sonny thought that things were going pretty well at this stage in his music career. He was married, with a baby daughter born in '71, and he was a working musician. He didn't have a lot of money, but overall life was pretty good.

Then, one beautiful fall day in November 1977, Marlon called Sonny out of the blue and asked if they could meet. Sonny drove over to Marlon's place at Alsab Farm Apartments and, as he was driving, Sonny wondered what it was that Marlon needed to talk to him about. And all he could possibly come up with was that things weren't going so well with Exile, and that Marlon wanted to re-join Doug and him in their newly formed band, The Breeding Bunch. After the disappointing sales of "Try it On," Exile went into a funk and didn't book a lot of local gigs, so Sonny thought they weren't doing too well as a band. Many people thought perhaps it was time for Exile to throw in the towel. Even though this assessment of the band wasn't too far off, Sonny still couldn't have been more wrong, on all counts.

As it turns out, Mike Chapman hadn't written them off entirely, as they had previously feared. In early 1977, Chapman had a great idea for a song and asked his partner Nicky Chinn, who was based in London, to get on a plane and fly to L.A. to write it with him, which Nicky immediately did. After it was finished, Chapman realized that Exile was the perfect band to record this new song, titled "Kiss You All Over." So even though they hadn't had a hit with "Try It On," Chapman still believed in them wanted them to make it big, and he just knew that this one would be a hit song for them. Chapman played "Kiss You All Over" for the band, they liked it, and it was decided that they would cut the record locally at Forum Studio in Crescent Springs, Kentucky, which was located in the Northern Kentucky/ Greater Cincinnati area.

At the meeting, Marlon explained to Sonny that Exile was currently in the studio working on an album called Mixed Emotions, produced by legendary producer/songwriters Mike Chapman and Nicky Chinn, but that they were having some trouble with their bass player, Danny Williams. Danny wasn't terribly happy with the disco direction that Chapman was leading the band in, and he and Chapman had clashed creatively on several occasions while in the studio. Basically, it appeared that the stress of recording had caused things to go sour between Danny and Chapman, and the band was worried that the disruptions might jeopardize their relationship with Chapman. As a whole they worried that they couldn't continue recording or playing with him, so they were looking for someone to replace Danny immediately. It was a pretty touchy situation: not only were they looking to replace a band member while in the middle of recording an album, but Danny and Steve Goetzman also happened to be best friends. By all accounts, Danny was a great bass player and harmony singer, and he had even written a couple of the songs on the new album. They were in a really tough spot with this decision.

At the same time, Danny saw the writing on the wall and decided to leave the band. He said he had been really unhappy with the changing direction of Exile's sound from rock to disco, and he didn't like that Chapman had wanted to change their sound so drastically. He was extremely disappointed that Chapman didn't see the "realness" of what Exile had to offer. Danny said he also felt that J.P., Buzz and Marlon had grown together during the recording process, while he increasingly felt more isolated. It is difficult to adequately describe the pressures a band faces when they go into the studio to record a new album: the excitement, the nerves, the creative differences on how each song should sound, egos, and time and money constraints are all factors. Danny left the band in December 1977, and in January 1978 the album dropped. Exile hired Sonny, and in an interesting twist, Danny went to take Sonny's place in Doug's band. It was daunting for Sonny to come in and replace Danny, who was a great musician and vocalist, especially in the midst of recording a studio album. But that's exactly what he did:

Sonny came in and finished recording the final two tracks on Mixed Emotions, and then immediately went on tour with them to support the album that would change all of their lives. Retrospectively, Danny said he got the best of both worlds because he was a part of that chart-topping album, and he received royalties for playing on the songs, yet he didn't have to go out and tour and do all the work associated with making that album a success. And he had nothing but praise for Sonny's playing and his ability to fit in seamlessly with the band.

Sonny recalled the first show he played as a part of Exile, which was at a high school gym in Eastern Kentucky. The band had bought the Winnebago to tour in, and it was large and comfortable. By this time they even had a roadie, Greg "Chipper" Peterson, to help with their gear. When they arrived at the venue and were getting ready to play, Sonny walked out on stage only to find that his amp had already been set up for him, his guitar was in its guitar stand, and a glass of water was sitting neatly on top of his amp. After all his years of playing with bands and sweating, hauling, setting, up and tearing down his own gear night after night, to see all of these things done for him, he nearly cried. It was truly a thing of beauty to behold. It was a brand new experience, and that's when he knew he'd hit the big time. For the first time in his career, all he had to do was show up and play. It was every musician's dream, and the dream just kept getting better and better.

One minor dilemma for Sonny, however, was salary. In 1977, each band member was paid just $75/week. But, because he had a wife and child, that amount simply wasn't enough for him to join the band and support his family. In fact, Sonny briefly considered quitting music, cutting his hair, and going to law school. He had been making decent money in Doug Breeding's band, and joining Exile at that time would have been a pay cut. So, the band held one of their special meetings and together they decided that, due to the extenuating circumstances (he was the only married band member, much less married with a little girl), they agreed to double his pay to $150/week. That money still wasn't great, but Sonny knew deep down that's what he wanted to do. Against the advice of his close friends Doug Breeding and Jerry Morse, he accepted. Fortunately for everyone involved, in just a few short weeks the single from that album would be released, and, for a while at least, the days of worrying over money would fall by the wayside.

On the Sunday after the album was finished, Nicky Chinn flew into Lexington's tiny Blue Grass Airport to get them to sign the production contract. It was the first time he had actually met the band, and it was all very exciting. After signing the contract, Nicky wanted to take the guys out for a drink. What he didn't know, however, was that Lexington had alcohol blue laws at the time preventing the sale of liquor on Sundays, so no bars or liquor stores were open at all on Sundays in Lexington. As Nicky so aptly stated, "The thought of NOT having a celebratory drink after signing a production contract was out of the question." So they drove over to the next state (which happened to be Ohio) and celebrated the night away. It was a dream come true for the guys, who had worked so long and so hard to get the album done and to get this deal. This time, they just knew that things would be different for them. And for once, they were right.

Exile decided that it was time to hire another full-time roadie. A young guy named Jeff Hunt had been around them for quite a while because his sister's band, Joshua Cooley, opened up for them on occasion. Even though Jeff was just a teenager, he loved hearing Exile play, and he would manage to sneak into the Richmond clubs to see them whenever he could. In fact, he was such a fan of the band that he was instrumental in getting Exile to play his high school graduation party back in '75. His graduating class raised a good bit of money that year, so when it came time to get a band to play for their end of the year party, Jeff told them there was only one band to get. Exile played one of the barns in Renfro Valley, and it was a huge party and everybody had a rockin' good time.

A couple of years later, Jeff was working with his sister's band opening for Exile at the annual Spring Break party they did down at the Safari Beach Motel in Daytona Beach, FL. While there, Exile offered the roadie job to Jeff for the same salary the guys were making themselves, $75 a week. He had been making $200-$250 with Joshua Cooley, so he told them:

Fellas listen, you know I'd love to, you're my idols, but I can't take a pay cut like that. But they kept after me and I finally did. Of course, it was a great time to join because within two months "Kiss You All Over" went #1, so it was just crazy from then on. I was just 20 years old.

They later hired another roadie named Billy Moore after Chipper left, and both Jeff and Billy were with them for many, many years. Everyone agreed that they were the best, hardest-working, and funniest roadies in the business. That first year, they went from playing high school dances and local bars to arenas and stadiums, learning as they went. With the release of *Mixed Emotions*, all of their lives were changed, almost in an instant. They were on fire.

Exile signed with illustrious Warner Bros. Records and landed a distribution deal with Curb Records. As soon as "Kiss You All Over" was released, it started burning up the charts. They first went into the studio in the fall of '77, and *Mixed Emotions* was completed in February '78.

"Kiss You All Over" was released in May. By September, that single had reached #1. It was what is commonly referred to in the music business as "an overnight sensation." One of the top managers of the day, Jim Morey, came and sought them out after a show in Houston, TX. He found them backstage and flat out told them that he wanted to represent them. Morey was a really big deal. He managed Dolly Parton and Neil Diamond, and he later went on to represent Michael Jackson in the late 80s and 90s, along with many other talented musicians along the way. Exile could not have been happier to agree for him to be their manager. They had a big record deal, a #1 hit, and a top music manager. They finally had everything they had ever wanted.

Soon they were called to fly out to Los Angeles to play on The Midnight Special, the biggest music variety show on TV at the time. The Midnight Special was different than other variety shows because they asked artists to actually play their instruments and sing their songs, versus lip-synching their way to a track for the performance. It was yet another really big milestone for them to get on the show. Upon their arrival at LAX, two limos picked them up and whisked them away to the infamous Continental Hyatt House on the Sunset Strip, where, in 1975, the iconic photograph was taken of Robert Plant clenching his fists and smiling triumphantly out over the balcony at all of Hollywood beneath him. It was a true rock-n-roll hotel that quickly became known as the "Riot House" for all the crazy things that happened while rock stars stayed there. While still in the limos (a first for all of them), Sonny LeMaire casually turned on the radio and heard the downbeat of "Kiss You All Over." He hopped out and started jumping up and down like a lunatic, yelling for the guys in the other limo to turn to the same radio station. It was a miraculous, stupendous, unreal moment, and it was all happening to THEM. Sonny said:

> It was one of those moments where you have listened to the radio all your life growing up, and all of a sudden there's your song being played on the radio. It was a pretty special moment.

Back in Lexington, on the night that The Midnight Special show with Exile as the guest aired, Doug Breeding was playing his usual set at the Terrace

Room in Lexington. At 11:30PM he stopped playing and told everyone to go on home and support their home-town band, Exile, and watch the show. The Breeding Bunch still had an hour and a half yet in their set, but Doug said goodnight, and that they would see everyone tomorrow. And with that, everyone went home. According to Doug, the whole town practically shut down so people could watch Exile on TV that night. The Kentucky fans' support of their guys was unwavering.

Exile played "Kiss You All Over" on live television that night for a national audience. At the end of the performance, J.P. and Stokley gave each other a high five. Fellow musician Greg Martin (from the Kentucky Headhunters) was watching the show that night, too, and he said it was like they were saying "Hey man, we finally made it!" He, along with all the fans back in Kentucky, was so proud of them. For the fans who had been with them from the very beginning, it was like a part of each and every one of them was on that stage performing with those boys. Everyone in the area felt like they were a part of Exile's success in becoming #1 recording artists, and the local fans felt a love and a pride that cannot properly be put into words. When Exile got home from L.A. there was a big party to congratulate them, and the guys were truly touched by the outpouring of love and support. These hometown boys had truly "done good."

"Good" doesn't even begin to describe what happened next. Due to the success of their hit single, "Kiss You All Over," Exile was chosen to be the opening act for Aerosmith on their world tour. A few of the guys had been around for the Caravan of Stars tour, which was a big deal back in its day, but this Aerosmith tour was like winning the rock-n-roll lottery. Marlon Hargis recalled what may have been the first stop on that tour playing Market Square Arena in Indianapolis, IN. The arena held about 16,000 people, and was by far the largest venue they had ever played. Sonny LeMaire's childhood friend, John Payne, had come to the show to support the band and was standing side stage with his camera, ready to capture every awesome moment of their performance for them. They had arranged the stage show so that Exile would come out onto a darkened stage, and then when they were announced the lights would go up, and there they would be, ready to rock.

They were all in their places when the announcer came on and asked the crowd to please welcome #1 recording artists... Exile! Not only did the intensely bright stage lights go up, but at that moment the crowd also lit their lighters and held them up as tribute (a quaint gesture that has now been replaced at concerts by holding up lit back screens of cell phones and waving them in the air today). The luminescence from all the lighters, coupled with the piercing stage lights, was so bright and so awesome that it was practically blinding. From the side of the stage, John Payne was so shocked by the intense glare that he dropped and broke his camera. The guys in Exile were stunned as well, but they smiled, stepped right up to the mics, and played their hearts out. They had gotten this far, and they weren't about to act like amateurs now. Stokley preened and strutted and jumped around the stage, and the crowd went wild. He was playing the role he had prepared for all these years: major stadium rock star. They were electrifying. Exile proved that they deserved to be there on tour with Aerosmith with each and every show.

The second or third night of the tour, their roadie Jeff Hunt was leaving Exile's dressing room and heading toward the stage, when Steven Tyler came walking by with a stack of t-shirts slung over his shoulder. He saw Jeff's laminated Exile pass and asked if he worked for Exile, to which Jeff replied in the affirmative. Tyler said he always gave the opening act some Aerosmith concert t-shirts, and asked if Jeff could take him back to Exile's dressing room to meet the guys and give them some shirts. Jeff was a huge rock-n-roll fan, and he was completely star-struck by Steven Tyler, but he wanted to act cool and make a formal introduction to the band. So he knocked on the dressing room door and said "Hey guys, Steven Tyler is out here. Is it ok if he comes in?" And the guys shouted, "Are you kidding?! Get him in here!" Jeff remembered him being really nice, and he came in and introduced himself and handed out t-shirts to each of the guys. That night on stage, Steven Tyler ran out to join them after one of their songs. He screamed out to the crowd "Kiss You All Over is #1 for four weeks in a row?" and with that he leaned over and stuck out his bony rear end and yelled "Well, kiss my ass!" And with that he ran off again. The guys cracked up and the crowd screamed and cheered. It was hysterical, but it also belied a certain truth:

Aerosmith was a huge rock-n-roll band who had sold millions of records, but up to that point they had never had a #1 hit, and Exile had. The guys were humbled and proud at the same time. They were able to do something that Aerosmith, with all their success, had not. Now that's truly saying something.

As the tour went on and they got to know each other a bit better, the guys from Aerosmith learned that the guys in Exile were from Kentucky. They were particularly curious if anyone in the band could get them something they had only ever heard about - moonshine. Shortly thereafter, a friend of the band from Eastern Kentucky brought in two one-gallon jugs of moonshine for Exile to give to them. That next night before the show, Joe Perry came up to them in a sad state and asked, "What was in that stuff?" To which Sonny replied, "It's pure grain alcohol," which can be as high as 80%. Perry said that it had nearly killed them the night before. Sonny asked, "Well how much did you drink?" It turns out the guys from Aerosmith had consumed the entire two gallons over the course of 24 hours. For anyone who has never before tried moonshine (and even those who have), they were extremely lucky to even be alive. It has been well documented that Steven Tyler and Joe Perry called themselves "The Toxic Twins," and perhaps this story was yet another reason for that moniker. Aerosmith managed to go onstage and perform that night, but for the life of them, the guys in Exile didn't know how.

After the Aerosmith tour ended, the next amazing gig for Exile was opening up for Heart on the last leg of their Dog and Butterfly tour. Jeff Hunt remembered Ann, Nancy and the rest of the band as being very nice, and they were incredible performers live. At their last show on the tour at Cobo Hall in Detroit, Michigan, lead singer Ann Wilson called the guys onstage and thanked them for being such a great opening act. Exile was so proud to share the spotlight with the members of Heart. When recently asked about what she remembered of those days touring with Exile, Ann Wilson wrote that "Kiss You All Over was one of the deepest sexy songs of the 70's in my opinion. What girl could not be convinced?" All these years later she remembered how great a song that was, and she wasn't alone. Recently, Billboard released The 50 Sexiest Songs of All Time, and "Kiss You All Over" was #9, right below

Rod Stewart's "Do Ya Think I'm Sexy?" People seem to love that song as much now as they did then.

Exile's ascent seemed unstoppable. They kept up the string of awesome gigs by next going on tour with Boston, which was also a great experience. Even those amazing arena-rock musicians and their fans loved "Kiss You All Over." Not every show went without its mishaps, however, and one night during that tour they were playing the Spectrum in Philadelphia, PA, and someone down front threw a bottle at the stage. It shattered, and a piece of glass hit Stokley right above his eye. Regardless of the blood dripping down his forehead, he never missed a beat. The band continued to play, and the show went on as usual. The band didn't even realize that anything was wrong. At the end of their set, Stokley came off stage and said he was bleeding. It just showed that no matter what, Jimmy Stokley and Exile would keep on rocking. They were true professionals, both then and now.

Soon they were called to go on England's Top of the Pops, the top music show in Great Britain.

"Kiss You All Over" had been a huge hit in the United States, and this show would make the song even bigger in Europe and the rest of the world. Nicky Chinn flew the guys to London on a Sunday, and that day they got a limo and visited all the top tourist attractions, like Buckingham Palace and the Tower of London. After a full day of seeing the sights they decided they would like to celebrate a bit, so they found a nearby hotel bar and ordered a round of drinks. But, in a strange twist that mirrored what had happened when they tried to go out for drinks on a Sunday in Kentucky, London had its own set of laws for serving liquor on Sundays. They were told that they could not be served a drink unless they were actually staying there at the hotel. So Nicky went and booked them a room, and once again they celebrated the night away.

On that trip to Europe, Mike Chapman and Nicky Chinn's new label, RAK Records, a subsidiary of EMI, flew them to Amsterdam to make their first music video. Nicky chartered a private plane for them, another first for the guys. It was the height of luxury. Nicky stocked the plane with Fortnum and Mason "food hampers," which were basically high-end picnic baskets filled with champagne and delicious snacks. They were getting the royal rock-star treatment. The only unfortunate part of all this was that Buzz Cornelison absolutely hated flying, and it didn't matter at all that he was in a private jet. He was ill practically the entire trip and couldn't enjoy the star treatment one bit. The other guys, however, made the most of every minute of it. They arrived in Amsterdam and made the music video, and took the jet back to the States, where they went back to L.A. and performed on a new music show called Solid Gold, which turned out to be hugely popular in the 80s. It featured attractive hosts and beautiful dancers in risqué, barely-there costumes. They weren't just on top of the pop charts; they were on top of the world.

But as the law of Physics states, what goes up must come down. Exile's follow-up single, "You Thrill Me," barely cracked the Top 40 back in the U.S. Their next album, *All There Is*, was recorded and released in 1979, but it failed to yield any hits. The first single from that album, "How Could This Go Wrong," went very wrong for them, and only peaked at #88 on the Billboard charts. Not to mention the fact that things had gone even worse for them while they were in the studio in L.A.

recording the album. All those years of screaming himself hoarse and singing improperly had taken its toll on Stokley's voice. Mike Chapman was again producing their album, and he was becoming increasingly frustrated with the quality of Stokley's vocal tracks. At one point, Stokley had been in the studio for 8 hours straight trying to get the vocals the way Chapman wanted them, and he just couldn't do it. Chapman was furious. He told Stokley to get out and he went and got Sonny LeMaire and told him to get in there and sing.

Sonny was completely freaked out. He was a backup vocalist, not a lead singer. But when Mike Chapman told you to do something, you did it. Sonny went in and did his best, but he couldn't quite get the vocals how Chapman wanted them, either. The stress and pressure was simply too much. Chapman was getting madder and madder, cursing up a blue streak. Finally, Sonny took off the headphones and walked into the sound booth. He told Chapman that he couldn't get vocals out of someone by acting that way. Chapman actually calmed down and apologized, and after that they were able to record the track. But the damage was done. Stokley only ended up singing a few lines here and there on the new album.

After that experience, Chapman vowed that he would never record with Stokley again. And that, unfortunately, was the beginning of the end for Jimmy Stokley as the lead singer of Exile. It was heartbreaking for them to see this happen to their friend, a guy who had put so much of himself into the band. Those years of screaming and partying had taken a toll, and even though it sounded great, it wasn't good for him in the long run. They agonized over the decision, but they knew they had to get a new lead singer.

Les Taylor was a singer/guitarist who had been playing in the Lexington music scene for a while. In fact, back in '65 or '66, he was playing with a band called the Ovations in Corbin, KY when they got a gig to play with The Exiles at the Martin Youth Center. Little did he know that years later he would be asked to join them. In July of 1979, Les was playing talent night at the Camelot on Alexandria Drive when J.P. walked in and pulled up a chair. He told Les that Exile was going to be making a change in the band, and asked him if the opportunity presented itself, would he be interested in joining them? Les said he sure would; when and what day and what time? And that was that. By late July, Les joined the band as singer and guitar player. He said he rehearsed with them for less than a week, and then on August 10, 1979, they all boarded a Learjet at Bluegrass Field to play the Illinois State Fair in DuQuoin, IL. There they opened for England Dan and John Ford Coley ("I'd Really Love to See You Tonight"). Les recalled:

> I was on Cloud 9 to say the least. It was a dream come true for me. I had always wanted to be a part of this group, and the fact that it was finally coming true, I was kind of pinching myself. We flew up on a Learjet and that was just awesome. Our show was at 8pm and I was sitting back in my apartment at 11:30 that night. Coming out of a club situation and into a national act and being on the national stage, it was a pretty awesome experience.

At the same time, Mike Chapman had arranged for a singer/songwriter/pianist from Tennessee named Mark Gray to come out to L.A. to audition to be in the band as well. It is believed that songwriter Jeff Silbar had recommended Mark to him. They flew Mark out to L.A. where he performed a gospel song for J.P. and Buzz at Chapman's palatial estate in Beverly Hills (which formerly belonged to Sir Paul McCartney). Mark was hired on the spot. Just like back in the earliest days, Exile had two lead singers: Les Taylor and Mark Gray. Mark did mention, however, that he always considered himself a songwriter first and foremost. In fact, he co-wrote several of Exile's biggest hits (even if some ended up being covered by other artists, as we will see later). Both he and Les started with the band on the same day, August 6, 1979, and their first gig was a mere four days later, on August 10th. They were thrown right into the mix and were off and running on a whirlwind of tour dates.

In the meantime, the second single from *All There Is*, a song called "Let's Do it Again," was released. It failed to even chart. The last single, "Too Proud to Cry," was released next. Nothing. The songs from this album were definitely more disco-sounding than rock, as were most of the top hits of the Billboard Top 100 for 1979: "Bad

Girls" by Donna Summer, "Le Freak" by Chic, and "Do Ya Thing I'm Sexy" by Rod Stewart, to name a few. But for whatever reason, Exile's follow-up songs just never caught on. It was like the old days all over again: they couldn't get a national hit single. Internationally, however, it was a whole other story. Exile entered the 1980s with international success, but back home in the states, their star was fading.

THE 80s

"Kiss You All Over" had been a global hit as well as a national hit for Exile. It went triple platinum (selling over 3 million units) in the US, and made the Top 10 (and usually the top 5) in countries like Canada, the United Kingdom, France, Austria, Germany, Switzerland, Holland, Sweden, Denmark, Norway, Belgium, New Zealand, Australia, Tokyo, and also in a seemingly unlikely place: South Africa.

As it turns out, Exile was really popular in Springbok, South Africa. "The Part of Me That Needs You Most" was a song from *All There Is* that was never released in the U.S., but it became a huge hit in both Europe and South Africa. Bands are always saying things like "We don't have a big following in the U.S., but we're huge in Belgium." Well, for Exile, it turns out that they were really popular in South Africa. On their tours there they were given the royal treatment. For example, when they arrived at the Springbok airport, fans and paparazzi were waiting, screaming, and holding banners. Mark Gray said it was like they were The Beatles or something, the way people went nuts when they arrived. Once again, they were experiencing a level of fame heretofore unseen by any of them previously. They were as far from home as they had ever been, but they were wholly embraced by the fans there. Even half a world away they were stars.

Mark said he had a lot of good memories from 1979-1982 while he was playing with Exile. In his words, they were "A bunch of guys playing music and traipsing around the world." Not bad work if you can get it! This Kentucky band had gone from local hometown heroes, to New York recording artists, to global jet-setting rock stars. Mark remembered the first time that they went to South Africa, and they stayed at the five-star Johannesburg Carlton Hotel. The venue they were playing was right across the street from the hotel, which is where they played 2 shows/night for 2 or 3 weeks straight. Their shows were so popular and the crowds liked them so much that soon they were asked back to play a nine-city tour all across South Africa.

There was, however, one scary situation from the first trip that arose while they were staying at the Carlton. Their rooms were up on the 12th floor, and they had a nice view of Johannesburg. Mark Gray woke up early one morning and was going to go out and enjoy the day when the phone rang. It was Sonny LeMaire telling him not to go anywhere, and to look out his window. Mark looked down to the street below and saw the red hats of the men in the South African army lined up outside the hotel. Just then, there was a knock at his door. A soldier with a rifle had come to Mark's room to tell him that they were being evacuated and to escort him from the building. Mark put on his shirt (luckily, he already had on his pants) and they headed for the elevators. They gathered in the lobby, and were told they could go back up to quickly to gather their personal effects. When they got up the 12th floor, there was a man sitting on the ground studying a large blueprint of the hotel. He had a large dog beside him. He told them they couldn't go back to their rooms anymore, so they went back down to the lobby where they were then ushered into a van outside the hotel. They were taken to their promoter's house outside the city, where they spent the afternoon.

Eventually they got word that they could come back to the hotel. The threat had been eliminated.

It was only then that they learned the precise nature of the reason for their evacuation: it seems a terrorist had booked a room on the 14th floor above them (there was no 13th floor), and he was going to blow up the hotel. The soldiers were able to get to him before he could deploy his bomb, and he was shot and killed. They were allowed to go back to their rooms that evening as if nothing happened. They played their show across the street that night as usual, but it was the only time that there were empty seats for their performance. By the following night things had returned to normal, and once again they played to a packed house. In the early 80s the world was becoming increasingly aware of the issue of apartheid, or racial segregation, that persisted in South Africa. The guys were safe, but the social and political issues there were made very real to them on that day.

I remember my dad being gone for what felt like an incredibly long time, but I never knew about the danger the band faced that day. All I knew was that I was a kid, and I missed my dad very much. I had grown up with him playing nights and weekends, and then touring and being gone a lot, but to have him gone for weeks at a time and so far away was very hard indeed. After school I would run to the mailbox, because every day he would send a pretty new postcard to me, and I treasured each and every one. But those weeks felt like at least a year to me, and I carried the hole in my heart from missing my father with me well into adulthood. Being a world-traveling rock-star is the goal of many a musician, but for families and children back home it can be less than ideal. The stresses, temptations and excesses on tour can rip families apart. Sadly, this time period created a rift that led to my dad and me growing apart in later years. That fracture in the relationship with my dad was reflected in the coming fractures and splits in the band as well. Soon after their return to the States, their career as a band got about as low as it could get. It was the beginning of the end of the rock-n-roll dream for Exile.

The early 80s were not kind to Exile back home. They had two more back-to-back disappointing albums with poor sales. In 1980 they released the album D*on't Leave Me This Way*, which contained the single "Take Me Down," written by J.P. Pennington and Mark Gray. Again, the album did well in Europe and South Africa, but it went nowhere in the U.S. Their next album, *Heart and Soul*, managed to do even worse. None of the new songs were catching on. Those high-rolling "Kiss You All Over" days seemed to be stuck in some distant past. They just couldn't get that magic back. After many great years Buzz Cornelison left the band for good in 1981, followed by Mark Gray in 1982. The remaining lineup for the band was J.P. Pennington, Les Taylor, Marlon Hargis, Steve Goetzman, and Sonny LeMaire. Those members would somehow remain intact through the next phase of Exile's long and illustrious career. But unfortunately, things had to get a whole lot worse for them before they got better.

The venues they played got smaller and smaller, and the gigs started to dry up. An old friend of the band, Pat Collins, came to their rescue and gave them a steady gig. Pat owned the Southland and Eastland Bowling Lanes in Lexington, KY, and each had lounges where local bands would play. The Rebel Room was the name of the lounge in Southland Bowling Lanes, and The Terrace Room was the one in Eastland. Both could hold about 150 people, and they each had a dance floor, so they were a pretty decent size for a local venue in Lexington. Pat hired Exile to play nightly as the house band at the Rebel Room in Southland Bowling Lanes on Jan 8, 1982. They had gone from playing arenas and stadiums to back to playing local bowling lanes, but they were just glad to have the work. Pat said he never would have been able to afford for them to play just a few years prior, so he was pretty happy with the situation because the local crowds still loved them. Those Kentucky and regional fans never let Exile down, and they never gave up on them, even when the guys in Exile were ready to give up on themselves. Pat said the year that Exile played as the house band drew the biggest crowds he'd ever had. The silver lining to Exile's situation was that Pat let them practice there during the day for free. This proved to be instrumental in the next phase of Exile's success, even though they couldn't have known that then. All they knew was that they were back to playing bowling alleys, and it felt like they were going nowhere fast.

During this low point in their careers, many of the guys had to get side jobs just to make ends meet. I remember my dad working day shifts at our friend Jerry Morse's pizza place, called J.J.

Jinglebottom's, which was over by Champ's roller rink, where I went skating every single weekend. I could go hang out with my dad, Jerry, and his sons after rolling skating, I got free pizza any time I wanted, and they had the very first upright arcade game, Space Invaders. It was a kid's paradise. I thought my dad was just helping his old friend with his new business; I didn't know how badly my family was struggling financially. In the meantime, Exile continued to play nightly at Southland Bowling Lanes, but they weren't terribly happy with the way things were going for them. It was a disheartening time, but somehow, like always, they stuck with it. Their devotion to making Exile work again was absolute. Sonny LeMaire told Michael Jonathon at a taping of Woodsongs Old Time Radio Hour in early 2013:

> The vision and the dream never died. And every time we got knocked back and knocked down, the thing about being in a band is that any one of us at different times could be kinda down, you know, worried about things. There was always somebody to pick the other guys up. That's the great thing about a band: the chemistry of it. And that's the way it was.

Every time we got knocked down, we just came back. We had the desire to fight and come back strong.

An idea was formulating on how to keep themselves afloat, and they started working on a new sound while they practiced those long hours at Southland Bowling Lanes. They knew their rock and pop career was pretty much over, but there was a light on the horizon. Perhaps they could re-invent their sound yet again, only this time as a country music act. They were a Kentucky band, after all. J.P. Pennington had deep roots in country music, not only from his early days playing with Clyde Foley, but also from his mother, Lily May Ledford, an accomplished fiddle player and founding member of the Coon Creek Girls. And, it was next to impossible to grow up in the region without at least a cursory appreciation of country music. Maybe this crazy idea wasn't as far-fetched as it seemed.

It is also worthwhile to mention that, in 1979, a country act called Dave and Sugar released a song called "Stay With Me" that J.P. had written. Exile hadn't included it on any album to date, but somehow Dave and Sugar got hold of it and recorded it, and it went all the way to #6 on the country charts. Then in 1982, another country artist, Janie Fricke, had a hit with a song written by two Exile members, Les Taylor and Mark Gray (and another writer, Shawna Harrington-Burkhart), called "It Ain't Easy Bein' Easy." Additionally, "Take Me Down," one of the singles from Exile's album, *Don't Leave Me This Way*, written by Mark Gray and J.P. Pennington, ended up being yet another huge #1 hit for country act Alabama, who released it in 1982. The writing wasn't just on the wall; it was everywhere, all around them. In a few short years, country artists were having hits with songs written by several members of Exile. They obviously had a knack for writing hit country songs, so why not play those songs themselves? So with that thought, every day they worked on writing and practicing their new material, then they would try it out on the crowds at the Rebel Room at night. And lo and behold, people liked it. They really, really liked it. And that is how, once again, Exile was re-born, only this time as a country music act. At that same taping of Woodsongs Old Time Radio Hour, Marlon Hargis recently reflected:

We all had the goal and the desire to keep going, to keep together. It wasn't fun going from playing arenas back to playing bowling alleys, but we also had a reason to do that - it was to work on songs for our country career. And I think we were successful at doing that.

That next year in February 1983 their old friend Doug Breeding hired them to be the house band for his successful Lexington club, Breeding's. Doug himself was sound mixer and light man for the shows. Breeding's catered more to a country music-listening crowd, and it was one of the most popular clubs in the region. The home-town crowd supported Exile's change from rock to country wholeheartedly. Once again, things were slowly starting to look up for the guys.

They suffered a minor setback, however, in August of 1983, when Huey Lewis and The News released their version of Exile's "Heart and Soul." It went to #1 on Billboard's Top Tracks, and to #8 on Billboard's Top 100. The guys in Exile were bewildered as to why it could be such a huge hit for Huey Lewis and not for them back when it was released, just a couple years prior, in 1981. When played one right after the other, the recordings of the two songs are almost the same. Huey Lewis added in a brief guitar interlude before the chorus at the end of the song, but otherwise they are practically identical. Everyone in Exile was happy that Huey Lewis got a hit with one of their songs, but it did hurt their pride just a bit that it hadn't happened for them. Of course, they later got to meet all the guys in Huey Lewis and The News, who couldn't have been a nicer bunch of fellas. But basically, that event was the nail in the coffin that seemed to confirm the fact that Exile's pop/rock days were over, and that it was time to move on to something else. They honed their new sound at The Rebel Room and at Breeding's, and they were finally ready to make a leap of faith.

During that year their manager, Jim Morey, introduced them to Buddy Killen, a Nashville Music Row legend. Buddy owned Tree Publishing and SoundShop Studios, and he was a respected, accomplished record producer and music publisher. Sonny was chosen to be the band emissary to play their new Exile songs for Buddy down in Nashville, and it was his job to convince Buddy that Exile could work as a country act. Fortunately, it wasn't too difficult a task; Buddy liked what he heard. As it turned out, Buddy also owned a popular steak house in Nashville called The Stockyard, and downstairs it had a lounge called The Bullpen where both established and up-and-coming country acts would play. Buddy agreed to let Exile play the The Bullpen lounge, and Jim Morey was then responsible for getting all the record executives he could gather to attend the shows, in the hopes that he could land Exile a country record deal.

Exile went down to Nashville and did two of these showcases, as they were called, but most of those in attendance didn't seem even remotely interested in giving them a record deal. Many of those record executives had a hard time seeing and accepting Exile as a country band. They feared that the Exile name was too associated with rock-n-roll and pop to successfully cross over to country. Not everyone felt that way, though. Two Epic A&R people, Bonnie Garner and Susan Burns, came to the first show. For the next one they brought along Rick Blackburn, head of Epic Records, a smaller division of Columbia. Rick must have seen not only their incredible talent but their fighting spirit as well, because he decided to go ahead and take a chance on them. He gave them their first country music record deal. Rick signed Exile to Epic Records and they went right into the studio. It's safe to say that they had never worked for anything so hard in their lives.

That year they released their first country album, simply titled *Exile*, with "The High Cost of Leaving" as the first single. "Leaving" was the first song written by J.P. and Sonny together, and the lyrics and music were meant to evoke legendary singer George Jones. Stylistically, it was a very classic country song. With Les Taylor on lead vocals, the song perfectly captured the down-home country sound they were aiming for. It took ten or twelve weeks, yet slowly but surely the song gained momentum, and ultimately "Leaving" made it all the way to #27 on the country charts. Finally, Exile had another hit! They were absolutely over the moon. Their country music career was off to a propitious start.

An interesting fact from that album (and every Exile album) was that, in the studio, the guys played their own instruments on all the songs, which was unheard of in Nashville at the time. It was standard practice for country recording artists to use studio musicians while recording. Pat McMakin was a young recording engineer who worked for Buddy Killen on their first country albums. He was surprised when the guys came in to the SoundShop to record their songs, because he was used to working with studio musicians to do the tracks, not the band itself. But right away, Pat knew they were onto something. He said that recording with them "felt very natural, very good." He also noted that "They brought such a wealth of experience into the studio, because they had already been superstars... So many people chase fame, that they forget to get talent along the way." This clearly was not the case for Exile. They trusted their gut, and made the record they wanted to make.

Exile knew that if they could pull off convincing Music Row that they could play on their own records that it would further define who they were as a band. Their gamble paid off. The second single from that album, the upbeat "Woke Up in Love," this time featuring J.P. Pennington on vocals, was released in 1984. It didn't take ten weeks for this song to catch on - it went straight to #1. Back in Lexington, their good friend Doug Breeding put a message up on the Breeding's marquee which read "Exile 'Woke Up in Love' #1." Doug even hosted a party in their honor at Breeding's, and so many people came out that there were traffic jams at the intersections from all the people trying to get into the place. As always, friends and fans came out of the woodwork to congratulate and support their very own hometown band, Exile, and their latest achievement. Five years after their first #1 hit, and one year into their country music re-invention, they had another #1 single. The guys were onto something big. They ran with it and never looked back.

To support that album, they toured with Grammy and Country Music Award-winning artist Ricky Skaggs. The only caveat to playing with Ricky was that they could not play their first hit, "Kiss You All Over." He did not think it was an appropriate song for his audiences. Even though they may have had misgivings about it at the time, in hindsight that was a good decision. In order for them to move forward it was necessary that they break with the past. That year they also went out and headlined clubs, theaters, and summer festivals on their own. Their momentum was building. That second summer after the release of *Exile* they played over 200 tour dates, which is a staggering amount of time to be out on the road. They were happy to be there, performing their songs, and doing what they loved most.

Along the way they'd play with and run into the more established country artists, and most were incredibly welcoming and supportive of the direction Exile was going in country music. But every once in a while they would encounter some resistance. There were a few country artists who thought that Exile didn't fit in to the country "establishment;" that perhaps they were even tainting what country music was all about. They called what Exile was doing "country pop." The guys didn't let it bother them one bit. It's true that the sound of country was changing, and Exile was changing right along with it. As always, when faced with adversity and negativity, they just went out and did what they did as best they could. There would always be critics, but the fans were eating it up, and they were happy with their success.

The last single from that album was called "I Don't Want To Be A Memory," written by J.P. and Sonny. It, too, went to #1, which was a first for them as a writing duo. They went on to write many more hits together over the years. J.P. described their mood after the release of "Memory:"

> We were ecstatic. I think we were even happier about the second #1 ["I Don't Want To Be a Memory], because it helped to validate that we weren't a flash in the pan. It proved we had songs that resonated on the radio and with the public. It cemented the fact that we had arrived, in what was a second career for us.

From then on and for quite a good period of time, it seemed like everything Exile touched turned gold. After much trial and error, they had finally found their sound. Those rock-n-roll exiles had come home to their Kentucky country roots, and it is there that they would stay.

Exile released their follow-up country album, *Kentucky Hearts, in 1984.* All three singles from that album hit #1: first, the infectious "Give Me One More Chance," then the more soulful "Crazy For Your Love," and finally, a song that is particularly special to me, called "She's a Miracle," which was released in 1985. "Miracle," written by J.P. and Sonny, has a pretty special backstory. J.P.'s wife, Suzie, was expecting their first child while he and Sonny were writing this song. J.P. had just found out that the child was to be a little girl. Sonny already had me, by then a not-so-little thirteen year-old girl. They were talking about how blessed they were to have and be expecting little girls in their lives, when the idea for "Miracle" came about.

2ND VERSE

I don't need to make the front page news

Or be the talk of the town

I don't need no wishing well

To throw my money down

I'm telling all the world I've got a heavenly girl

Right here on the ground

CHORUS

She's a miracle, a sight to see

Oh, the way she touches me

Way down deep, in my soul

Something's got a hold and it won't let go

If I stumble, if I fall

She's waiting right there to catch me

Oh, she's a miracle, a miracle to me

Jessie Rose Pennington was born, healthy and happy, the week of July 6th, the same week that song went to #1. What a very special thing for two fathers to do for their daughters: to write a song for us that wound up going all the way to #1. And even though she wasn't born yet, this song is also about my little sister, Chloe. The beauty of a song like "Miracle" is that it can be about any special woman or girl. That summer I got to go with them out to L.A. to watch them shoot the music video, which was an awesome experience. That song caught on like a fever, and Exile's meteoric rise was in full swing. 1984 was an incredible year for the band.

Due to their new-found chart-topping success, Exile was asked to come on the top country variety show Hee-Haw, where they performed both "Miracle" and "It'll Be Me." For that episode they even got to join the infamous sketch comedy portions of the show, "The cornfield" and "Pfft! You was gone!" It was a dream working alongside such talents as Buck Owens, Roy Clark, and Minnie Pearl. Exile was fortunate enough to be asked to appear on Hee-Haw several times over the years, in seasons 17, 18, 19 and 24. The guys had the time of their lives laughing it up with the talented members of the cast of crew, and they had an absolute blast every single time they went on the show.

Next, Exile was invited to perform at the Grand Ole Opry for the first time. It almost goes without saying that playing the Grand Ole Opry is the absolute pinnacle of country music. It is an honor and a huge achievement. They were now officially in the country music big time! It was very exciting, and they couldn't have been happier. But, it wouldn't be an Exile story without some bumps along the way. That day they were supposed to record two shows back to back, with two songs for each show. They chose to play "Woke Up in Love," their first #1 country song, followed by "I Don't Want To Be A Memory." They were so excited for this opportunity, just a bundle of nerves, but they were going to go out there and give it their all. When it was time to go on, Jim Ed Brown, the announcer, gave them a glowing introduction. They played both songs flawlessly and got a great ovation from the crowd. Everything went perfectly! They walked offstage feeling on top of the world.

They had a little time to kill before the next show, so they went back to the green room to relax, hang out and grab a quick bite to eat. Unbeknownst to the rest of the band, however, Steve Goetzman wasn't feeling so well after the set, so he went outside to get some fresh air. For some reason, which none of them can quite remember now, during the break they decided to change the order of the songs for the second show, so that this time they would play "Memory," followed by "Woke Up in Love." I guess they never heard the term "If it ain't broke, don't fix it." Steve came back in the room before it was time to go on, and they never even realized he hadn't been there when the decision to switch the order of the songs had been made. That is, until it was way, way too late.

Soon it came time to do the second show. Again, Jim Ed gave the outstanding introduction, and Exile went back onstage. Steve started counting off the beat, and instantly the other guys knew something wasn't right. They were expecting a straight 4-4 count for "Memory," when instead Steve was giving the 8th note shuffle count for "Woke Up in Love." Steve had started playing one song, while the rest of the band was playing another. They were smiling like crazy out at the audience and trying to pretend like this debacle wasn't happening, all the while shooting each other panicked looks and trying to figure out what exactly they were going to do. It felt to each of them like it went on forever, when in actuality it probably only lasted 15 seconds or so. By this time they had all figured out what had happened;

that for some reason Steve was playing the other song. Steve, too, had figured out the problem, and just like that, he switched to "Memory," while the rest of the band simultaneously switched to "Woke Up in Love." They couldn't have planned it better had they tried. It was a complete and utter disaster. Sonny remembered looking out at the audience and seeing that they all had a really strange expression on their faces. He happened to locate the face of J.P's wife, Suzie, amongst the crowd. She had a look of complete horror mixed with disbelief. He could only imagine what it sounded like to everyone out there, just a bunch of garbled noise, and he was so mortified all he could think about was wanting to find something to crawl under and hide. After what seemed like an eternity, J.P. shouted "Woke Up In Love!" and counted off the beat, and they all got on the same page and went into the song. Somehow, they managed to pull it together to finish playing the songs, but it was without a doubt the worst performance of their entire career. And it had happened to them at the Opry.

It was all they could do to make it through that second song and finish the show. They practically ran off stage when they were done.

Back in the green room they were all yelling at one another and almost threatening physical violence. They wanted to kill each other. After some time they were slowly able to re-construct what had happened, and they realized that Steve had not been in the room when the decision was made to reverse the order of the songs. They really should have known he wasn't there, but somehow, they just didn't. Needless to say, they weren't asked back. In fact, Exile didn't play the Grand Ole Opry again for 14 long years, until they were finally asked to play there again 2008. Several members have said they've heard a recording of that fateful show, and it was flat-out awful. Hilarious now, but still painful. Every band has a performance or two that they wish could be erased forever, and this was theirs. But, as always, they carried on with a smile on their face and a song in their heart. They continued touring and making (other) audiences happy.

It was a fairly large production at this point to take Exile on all those tour dates and keep them running on schedule. By this time they had two huge tour buses, two drivers, and several roadies, including Jeff Hunt and Billy Moore. Back in 1979 they had hired a friend of Sonny's named Raymond Patrick to be guitar tech for J.P. Pennington. Raymond went on to become their road manager, and served as promoter and business liaison between Jim Morey and the band during the tours in South Africa. He stayed with them during the days at the Rebel Room, and he was there to see them rise again in the country music business. Raymond had nothing but praise for the crew, and especially for Jeff and Billy, whom he called "consummate roadies." He said they loved what they did, and they were great to work with. Raymond added that everyone in the crew during those early country years, from the drivers, to the concession people, to the road crew, they were all really great people, and perhaps most importantly, the entire crew worked together to look after Exile's best interests. It could at times be difficult to manage the various personalities and egos of a top touring country act, but that crew always did an amazing, professional job. The road crew kept the guys up and running smoothly during the busiest, most successful portion of their career.

Exile's crew continued to grow, and in 1984 Raymond hired Clarence Spalding to manage the production crew. Spalding had a long history with Exile even prior to working with them. He was originally from Lebanon, KY, and he grew up listening to The Exiles. He even remembered sneaking in to Club 68 to see them when he was about 16 years old. Back in high school Spalding took a Journalism class, and for one of his assignments he chose to interview Kenny Weir and Buzz Cornelison. Exile later came and played one of his high school dances. One of the things he remembered most, though, was how fantastic a showman Jimmy Stokley was. According to Spalding:

> Stokley would come out in these skin-tight catsuits, and he was jumping up on speakers. People just didn't do that back then. It was a big, big show for a small town.

In 1978, while Spalding was in college, "Kiss You All Over" became a big hit. A few years later he became a manager at Breeding's, and when Exile was back in Lexington playing The Rebel Room at Eastland Bowling Lanes he would sometimes close early and go and watch them play. He was instrumental in getting their house gig at Breeding's during the early days of their country reinvention. The guys in Exile told him that as soon as there was an opening, they would find a job for him and take him out on tour with them. After they had a couple country hits under their belt, that's exactly what they did. Spalding left Breeding's and went on tour with them and never looked back. On the road, Raymond Patrick would ride with the band in one bus, while Spalding rode with the crew in the other. Spalding later worked his way up to being their tour manager when Raymond left in 1985. He summed up the experience of working with Exile like this:

> The great thing about being part of a band is being part of a brotherhood. We rode the buses together, and we went places together. Not only did I work for them, but we became friends. Their highs were my highs, and their lows were my lows. I got to be a part of that.

One of the highs of being with Exile then going out in support of the *Kentucky Hearts* album. That summer they toured with future male vocalist of the year Lee Greenwood, and also the amazing Oak Ridge Boys, who won Country Group of the Year, Single of the Year, and a Grammy for their hit song "Elvira" over the course of 1981 and 1982. A new mother-daughter act called The Judds would sometimes open for Exile on some of their early tour dates. In a funny twist of fate, as The Judds' star rose with hit after amazing hit, Exile ended up opening for them on their tours. The guys in Exile were always thrilled to play with all of these exceptionally talented individuals. They formed friendships with their fellow musicians on those tours that have lasted to this day.

One of the high points for me personally was in January of 1985, when I was lucky enough to get to go with my dad and Exile to attend one of the biggest nights in all of music, the American Music Awards, in Los Angeles. 1985 was such a huge year in pop, rock, and country music, and many the biggest names honored at that award ceremony for pop music are still known today: Lionel Richie, Cyndi Lauper, Prince, Bruce Springsteen, Tina Turner, Darryl Hall & John Oates, the Pointer Sisters, and Huey Lewis & The News. The King of Pop, Michael Jackson, was in attendance that night, as was an up-and-coming Madonna, whose film and music for "Desperately Seeking Susan" would come out later that year and thrust her into super-stardom. Representing the country music side for the American Music Awards was some of their biggest heavy-hitters: Kenny Rogers, Barbara Mandrell, Ricky Skaggs, Dolly Parton, the Oak Ridge Boys, The Judds, and, of course, Alabama. During the rehearsal, award ceremony, and the after-party, I met many of these amazing and talented artists. It was a magical evening being around so many people who were already or would later become legends, not only in their own genres, but in the music world as a whole.

Our seats for the ceremony just happened to be right in front of Canadian heart-throb Corey Hart, of "Sunglasses at Night" fame, who I had a huge crush on. We were across the row from the inimitable Pointer Sisters, who came over to talk to us during the rehearsal. Everyone was so nice! The next night during the award show, Prince did a moving and theatrical performance of "Purple Rain," and I was absolutely in teenage pop heaven. At the end of the show, all the nominees and winners were asked to come up on stage to join in for one last song. People from the front rows started pouring up onto the stage as well, and my dad took me up with him. I was practically standing beside Cyndi Lauper, whom I adored, and we were surrounded by all the other amazing artists of the day. I was completely and utterly star-struck. We later found out that many of the pop artists listed above left the after-party early that night to go into a studio with Quincy Jones to record the vocals for "We Are the World," a charity song that helped define the 80s, and brought further attention to the plight of hunger in Africa.

Clarence Spalding wasn't as thrilled as I to be on this trip, however. Members in both Exile and the Judds had teenage girls at the time, and he was in charge of looking after us. Ashley Ciminella is Naomi Judds' daughter with Michael Ciminella, and Wynona is her half-sister. Ashley and I happened to go the same school in Lexington, KY, and over the years we got to attend several different award ceremonies together with our parents, which was great because we were close in age and could hang out together. Back then Ashley was nicknamed "the unsung Judd," a play on words, because she was the family member who didn't sing. Ashley, however, grew up to do very well in her own right, albeit outside of the music world. She dropped her father's name and became the Ashley Judd we know and love from stage and screen. But back then we were just a couple of young teenage girls in need of supervision, so for the American Music Awards Spalding was tasked to look after us and cart us around from the hotel to the awards show venue, and back again. At that moment, he said, he wondered if his permanent job in Exile would be spent as a glorified babysitter, chasing after a couple of kids all the time. Fortunately, I don't think we gave him all that much trouble, and the award ceremonies were always a lot of fun for us.

In the mid-to-late 80s Exile was nominated for several awards, including the Academy of Country Music Awards and the Country Music Awards. They were nominated for Vocal Group of the Year, Song of the Year, and Album of the Year in that time period. They never won, but as they say, it was an honor just to be nominated. As I mentioned, Ashley Judd and I went to a couple of these country music award ceremonies with our parents, and Exile couldn't have been more happy for The Judds for all their multiple wins for

Vocal Duo of the Year and Single of the Year. The guys in Exile were just happy that they were able to have #1 songs, hit albums, and successful tours. In all, Exile achieved 13 country music nominations, and three gold albums. Those were impressive times for the guys, and they thought things couldn't possibly get any better. And then tragedy struck.

Jimmy Stokley died that year, in August 1985. He had been in declining health in recent years, and his heart finally gave out from a massive heart attack. The year before, Exile had performed at a fundraiser at Eastern Kentucky University to help Stokley with his mounting medical bills. They were shocked to see their once vibrant front man in such a state of physical decline. Not long after the fundraiser, Jimmy Stokley passed away. After the funeral service their old friend and former band member, Billy Luxon, invited them all to come over to his bar, J Sutter's Mill, to mourn and to celebrate the life of the their dearly departed friend. Mack Davenport and other early band members came up for the services and joined them at the impromptu wake. They had a heart-felt reunion of sorts, and took turns sharing their favorite stories of Stokley's days as both their good friend and formidable lead singer. Buzz Cornelison attributed all of their early success to him:

> I have to believe that nothing else would have happened had Stokley not been that initial stimulus. You can go into the writing the group did, the harmonies, the arrangements, the versatility, but that never would have shown if Stokley's demeanor and aura hadn't brought attention to the group.

Jimmy Stokley was fearless. They laughed as they remembered a time back in the early years, on one cold day on tour up north, when their old manager Jack Nance bet him $20 that he wouldn't jump into the outdoor hotel pool. It was cold, and they could see ice forming around the edges of the pool. Stokley didn't hesitate. He took a running start and jumped in. Jimmy Stokley lived life in just that manner - he jumped right in feet first and made a huge splash with his performance. To this day he is missed by all who knew him.

Exile went on to release *Hang On To Your Heart* later in 1985, and the #1 hits just kept coming, starting with the first single of the same name. That summer their tour manager Raymond Patrick's daughter, Shira, and I went on tour with them on the bus for a trip down to Orlando, Fl. The tour bus was huge and really nice: it had a front living room area with TV, a kitchen, a back lounge area, and bunk beds for all. Away we went from Kentucky down to Florida, where our destination was for Exile to play Disney World.

At one of the stops along the way we ended up in the same hotel as Charlie Daniels and his band. During the day Shira and I were free to roam around and swim at the hotel pool or otherwise keep ourselves occupied, while the band slept in or did sound checks. That day we got in the elevator to go downstairs and check out the hotel to see if it had a pool. A couple of floors down the elevator doors opened, and a large man with an even larger cowboy hat stepped in with us. In his hand he held a lasso. An honest-to-goodness cowboy lasso. He looked at us through his mirrored sunglasses and drawled, "I have some calves back home that need wrangling, so I'm going to the field out there beside the hotel to practice my lassoing. Would either of you fillies like to help me out? You just run and I'll try to lasso you." Now, I am a year or two older than Shira, and evidently a bit more cautious. I stayed silent, but she piped up and said, "Sure!" So, we all got out of the elevator together and walked over to the open field beside the hotel.

As crazy as this sounds, we did it. We were out in the open, on a warm, fine summer day, and we ran our legs off while the man attempted to lasso us. Meanwhile, up in his room, Exile's roadie, Jeff Hunt, remembered waking up and sleepily looking out his hotel window, only to see what turned out to be Charlie Daniels trying to lasso the teenage daughters of two of his bosses. He almost had a heart attack. Wide awake now, Jeff threw on some clothes and raced downstairs. He tried to appear nonchalant as he came strolling up to us and told us to wrap it up, because it was time to go meet our parents at sound check. The man thanked us for our help and that was that. It wasn't until Jeff told us the man was Charlie Daniels that we realized exactly how funny the whole thing was. In all fairness, there was a lot more running than roping going on; Mr. Daniel's lassoing skills were more miss than hit.

That wasn't the first (or the last) time Jeff or Exile's other roadie, Billy Moore, had to do babysitter duty while I was around. It couldn't have been easy having a teenage girl around a bunch of musicians and roadies all the time, but Jeff and Billy did a great job keeping me out of harm's way, and they never acted like I was a bother. Of course, years later I learned that my dad had made them swear they would keep me out of trouble or they would have hell to pay. Those poor guys! I must have been a handful. So thank you, Jeff and Billy; you are both princes among men.

We soon made it to Disney World and stayed at the Contemporary Resort, which had a monorail connecting it to the theme park. We could go from the hotel to the park in minutes, any time we liked. Exile was slated to play Disney's "Grad Nite," which is their free annual party for all graduating senior high school students. It is closed to outside visitors for that one night, and for Shira and me, it was the most fun show we had ever been to. We had the run of the park, there were no lines, and there were tons of kids close to our our age to hang out with. I remember riding Space Mountain three times in a row, just because we could. We also got to see the maze of interconnected tunnels beneath Disney World, which is where the dressing rooms are located. Park employees and performers zip around in golf carts in those tunnels to get from one side of the park to the other quickly, and without being seen. I have been to Disney World many times, but that was definitely the most magical time of all. In all, that summer's tour was a great success, which only presaged the amazing successes still to come for Exile. Their star continued to rise, and it would only go higher.

Exile was next asked to appear as musical guest on the top late night show in the country, The Tonight Show, with legendary host Johnny Carson. It just didn't get any bigger than that. I got to accompany my dad on that trip to L.A. as well. The guys were so excited - not only was Johnny Carson a living legend, but they also greatly respected and admired the Tonight Show Band with Doc Severinsen and Ed Shaughnessy. Steve Goetzman revealed that playing The Tonight Show was one of the top experiences he ever had in his many years with Exile, and he observed, "You played that show and there was no disputing you were a star. At the time, that was the pinnacle."

I watched back in the green room while they played their hearts out. Their only disappointment was that they didn't actually get to meet Carson. Exile was the musical guest, but they were not being interviewed for the show. After so many years as host, Johnny Carson had the timing of the show's recordings down to a science; his schedule was like clockwork. He only came onto the lot when it was time to go to make-up and then he went straight onto the set of the live show. If you weren't an interviewee, chances were you would never even get to really see him. The guys treasured that experience nonetheless. Les Taylor also confirmed that being on The Tonight Show was one of his favorite Exile memories. He said, "There again it was just one of the many dreams that have come true since I've been with the band." The Tonight Show was iconic, and it helped cement their status as national country music stars.

Exile had an amazing couple of years following their Tonight Show appearance. "I Could Get Used to You" came out in 1986, followed by the soulful "It'll Be Me." Both went to #1. In the interim, their label thought it would be a good idea to also release a Greatest Hits album, featuring the six amazing #1 hits they had recently had, and their first #1 from the rock days, "Kiss You All Over," plus a couple of new songs. One of those new songs was a little ditty called "Super Love," written by J.P. and Sonny. It was funky, humorous, and a little silly, and it went to #14 for them.

There is an interesting reason why perhaps that song didn't go to #1 as well. As I mentioned previously, when Exile initially crossed over into country music they had their detractors. Some said that their music wasn't "really country;" that it was just "country pop." Well, whatever it was, people sure seemed to like it, and they were happy with the music they were making. When they released "Super Love," a certain program director up at W4, a big country station in Detroit, decided that it just wasn't country enough. He wouldn't let his djs play it; so therefore, "Super Love" didn't get airplay in a major U.S. market.

The impact was definitely felt, as evidenced by the song not going all the way to the top of the charts. But you can't tell the fans that "Super Love" isn't a #1 hit, because to this day when they play it, it brings down the house. That song has been a high point in their live show for quite a while now.

The final single from *Hang On To Your Heart* came out in 1987, called "She's Too Good To Be True," which rounded out four solid #1 hits from that album alone. They had an incredible string of hits from 1984 -1987: nine #1 songs. But if there's one predictable thing about Exile, it's that just when things are going great and they are on top of the world, something happens and they come crashing back down. Success has a funny way of taking good situations (and sometimes even good people) and turning them on their ear.

After *Hang On To Your Heart*, things once again started spiraling downward for Exile. And this time, it looked certain that they would not be able to recover. One of the first indicators that all was not right within the band was when Marlon Hargis left in 1986, for a variety of reasons. A keyboard player named Lee Carroll was hired to take his place. Exile knew Lee from back in 1983 when he played with The Judds while they were touring together. Lee, of course, had known of Exile for much longer. His first concert had been to see Paul Revere and the Raiders on the Dick Clark Caravan of Stars tour in Bowling Green at Western Kentucky University in 1968 when he was just 15, and The Exiles were the opening act. Lee ended up attending Berkley College of Music in Boston, but he longed to be back closer to home, so he moved to Nashville to see if he could catch a break and play with some of the great artists there. Pretty soon thereafter he was hired to go out on tour and play keyboards with The Judds, and the rest is history.

As it so happened, Exile was playing a show with The Judds in Florida when J.P. came up to Lee and asked him if he would like to join Exile. He would be able to be a part of the band and make records with them and be involved in creative decisions, as opposed to being a keyboard player for hire, so the decision was a no-brainer for Lee. Exile was doing great! As with all new band members, they threw him in right away to play a gig at a rodeo in Oklahoma. Lee said he had a lot of anxiety playing that first show, but that it went ok, and after that everything was smooth sailing. He was an actual member of a successful band. But, Lee could also remember those not-so-long-ago days when Exile was playing the Rebel Room at Southland Bowling Lanes, and he had seen them go from high to low once before. It is doubtful he thought that cycle would happen again so soon, much less while he was with them. For all intents and purposes, Exile was still on top. But underneath that layer of success, things weren't quite as good as they seemed.

They released *Shelter from the Night* in 1987, and the first single, "I Can't Get Close Enough," shot to #1. In total, they had ten #1 hits from that era, an absolutely incredible achievement. From all outside appearances Exile still had the Midas touch, but internally, things were falling apart. Egos, in-fighting, and the stress from constant touring was taking its toll. The dynamics of keeping a band of five different personalities together is a precious, fragile thing. If that chemistry gets at all out of whack, bad things can happen. As a result, J.P. and Les, who had taken turns as lead singers on all of their recent hits, were in the process of deciding that they each wanted to pursue solo careers. Les left the band first and went on to release two solo albums under the Epic record label, *That Old Desire,* and *Blue Kentucky Wind.*

In the midst of all this upheaval, the next single from *Shelter* was released, a song called "Feel Like Foolin' Around." Basically, it tanked. It only made it to #60 on the Billboard country charts. After ten consecutive #1 hits, this was a serious blow to the band, which was only exacerbated by the fact that they had just lost one of their charismatic lead singers. But they picked themselves up, shook it off as best they could, and kept playing their tour dates. The show, after all, must go on.

Paul Martin was brought in to replace Les on vocals and rhythm guitar in 1988. Paul had grown up in Central Kentucky, so he knew of Exile, but of course it was their hit song "Kiss You All Over" when he had first heard them on the radio. His father was a musician and had his own studio, and Paul had been raised around instruments all his life. He was considered a bit of a wonder kid - he could play almost any instrument he picked up. When Les left the band, Paul was playing with Billy Joe Royal, who happened to be a friend of Doug Breeding's. When Doug heard that Les had left Exile, he mentioned Paul's name to Clarence Spalding, their tour manager. Spalding listened to Paul's demo and thought he just might be a good fit for the band. Exile was playing a show at Breeding's in July, and they asked Paul to come by so they could talk and get a feel for his personality.

Only a couple of weeks had passed before they asked Paul to come down to meet them again at the SoundShop Studios in Nashville. They told him that they had listened to his demo, and they thought the meeting at Breeding's had gone really well. Paul definitely had the talent and the right disposition to join the band. They weren't interested in holding auditions for a new lead singer; they were ready to make a decision. They simply asked him: "What are you doing for the rest of your life?" Paul said he was extremely flattered at being asked so quickly to join the band. He practiced with them for a couple of weeks before their first show, which was at a fair up in Wisconsin. He was a natural fit with Exile, and the show went well.

But then, just four months later, J.P. left the band to try his hand at a solo career. He went on to sign with MCA Records and release an album in 1991 called *Whatever It Takes*, with the singles "Whatever It Takes," and "You Gotta Get Serious." Exile had just lost both their lead singers within months of each other. It was like a bomb went off, and their world was suddenly turned upside-down.

It went down like this: Paul joined Exile in August of '88, and he was engaged to be married in three months' time. When he came back from his honeymoon in November, he was immediately asked to come to a band meeting. He worried, "Oh no! I just joined the band. What are they going to do? Fire me?" When he arrived at the meeting at the Hyatt in Lexington, he saw Steve Goetzman, Sonny LeMaire, Lee Carroll, and their agent, Jim Morey. Paul asked innocently enough, "Where's J.P.?" To which Sonny replied, "Sit down, Paul." Only then did he find out that J.P. had left the band. And, as if that weren't shocking enough, it had also been decided that Sonny and Paul would be the new lead vocalists. It was a pretty devastating blow to the band to lose both Les and J.P., their long-standing lead singers, and they had to scramble to find a viable solution. They all hoped and prayed that it would work.

Paul remembered very well that first show Exile did with Sonny and him on lead vocals. Sonny later told him that just before they were to play, he looked over across the stage at Paul and could see his hands visibly shaking. It was a pretty terrifying moment for all of them. This was make it or break it time, and they simply weren't sure they were going to be able to pull it off. It is impossible to overestimate just how much pressure was on Paul and Sonny from that moment forward. They were attempting to sing songs that J.P. and Les, two incredibly talented singers, had previously sung the lead vocals. Yet Exile continued to play their tour dates and carry on the best they could. In hindsight, Sonny said he couldn't believe they even tried. But try they did, and they managed to keep Exile going during this extremely difficult and challenging time.

They followed up "Foolin' Around" with the release of a song called "Just One Kiss," which made it to #9. What a relief! While it wasn't back to the #1 business as usual they had come to expect when J.P. and Les were with the band, it was still a top ten hit. But in reality, the damage was done. Their confidence was shaken. They managed to hang on to the hope that things would work out just fine, but the dream for them had turned into a nightmare. The last single from that album, "It's you Again," went to #21 - not an abject failure by any means, but not a top 10, or even a top 20 hit, either. Essentially, Exile was coming apart at the seams. Epic, their record label, lost confidence in their ability to make another hit record and dropped them. It looked like the end of Exile for good.

Somehow, Steve, Sonny, Lee and Paul were determined to keep the band going, even through what appeared to be insurmountable adversity. They quickly realized, however, that in order to replicate the intricate three-part harmonies of their biggest hits, they needed to hire another singer. In 1989, Mark Jones was brought in to play guitar and sing harmony with Sonny and Paul. Mark, another Kentuckian, was originally from Hopkinsville. Back in high school he was in charge of hiring the band for his class prom, and of course his first choice was to get Exile to play, but he was disappointed to learn they weren't available on that particular date. Mark was at the Nashville Pop Festival In 1972 when he heard Exile play live for the first time. Back then they were still just a regional act, and Mark recalled that they more than held their own against the big national acts that headlined the show. Mark said that they did a fantastic job, and he was very impressed with their professionalism and showmanship. Fast forward to 1980, and Mark was playing in a band with none other than future Exile keyboard player, Lee Carroll. Mark met Clarence Spalding at that time because Spalding managed the club where they were playing, Breeding's. Lee and Mark went their separate ways but always remained friends, and Lee was later hired to play keyboards in Exile. When it came time for them to hire a new guitarist/vocalist, Lee suggested his old friend and former band-mate, Mark Jones.

Mark knew going into it that Exile was in a rough place. They had lost their deal with Epic and they had sagging record sales. But, the one thing they had going for them was they still had a calendar-full of tour dates. Mark was originally hired not as a full member of the band, but rather as a musician to fill in and play those tour dates with them. He played guitar and fit in with the guys so well, though, that soon they asked him to fully join the band. This latest iteration of Exile survived through the end of the 80s, a decade of huge egos, extreme overindulgence, great fame and crushing loss. They saw incredible highs and terrible lows, both personally and professionally. The 90s were upon them, and even with all their indomitable optimism, their future was anything but certain.

THE 90s

Steve Goetzman, Sonny LeMaire, Lee Carroll, Paul Martin and Mark Jones got right to work writing new music, finding a new record label and recording a new album. They were each writing songs, trying to find their sound. They managed to get hooked up with well-known talent manager and executive, Tim Dubois. Tim must have seen that do-or-die Exile tenacity, because he agreed to sign them to the fledgling Arista Nashville label. They went into the studio and recorded the new material they'd been so feverishly working on. Exile had a lot to prove at this point, and they knew that this album could make or break them. They named the album *Still Standing*, and it was a testament to their sheer willpower and state of mind at that time. Their first single was written by Sonny and J.P. Pennington, with whom Sonny continued to write even though they were no longer bandmates. The song was called "Keep it in the Middle of the Road." It opened with some good old-fashioned finger-picking by Paul Martin, who sang lead vocals on the track. It was a surprisingly lively, optimistic song:

CHORUS

Keep it in the middle of the road, honey,
let's keep it in the middle of the road

Neither right nor left, right down the center
we go

Don't let our love fall by the wayside like a
lot of people I know

Whatever we do let's keep it in the middle
of the road

1ST VERSE

Honey, let's stay on the straight and narrow

Let's stay together just like a bow and
arrow

We're heading in the right direction, don't
lose control

Don't look, don't ever look back, 'cause
honey don't you know we're on the right
track

We've got a combination too good to let go

REPEAT CHORUS

Paul did a great job on guitar and vocals, and he played the steel guitar solo as well. Lee's excellent keyboard playing was also prominently featured on that track, Steve's drum beats were as solid as a rock, and the harmonies were simply superb. "Keep It in the Middle of the Road" was a hopeful, positive song, and they were rewarded for their hard work. In 1990, it went all the way to #17 on the charts. That experience was validating, energizing, and quite frankly, almost miraculous. A lot of bands wouldn't have been able to come back from losing their lead singer(s), losing their record deal, and almost losing their minds along the way. A lot of bands don't have the longevity that Exile has had, either.

Their success came at a difficult time for Paul, however. Around the time when he joined the band, his dad suddenly lost his corporate job of over twenty years. His mother was having some health problems, but she didn't want to worry her husband in this time of crisis so she kept her fears to herself. By the time Paul's sisters convinced their mom to go ahead and go to the doctor, she was diagnosed with advanced stage III breast cancer. She told Paul not to worry, that she was going to stick around long enough to see him have a hit record. Sadly, she passed away in June of 1989, and the song was released in November. It rose to the top 20 in early 1990. It was an exciting time, but also very bittersweet for Paul. He had achieved his goal of having a hit record, and his mom would have been so proud, but he was unable to share that accomplishment with her. The guys were very supportive of him in his time of loss and grief, and he managed to continue playing superbly night after night with the band.

Paul wasn't the only new band member to experience tremendous personal hardship during those years. Lee Carroll, too, had his own challenges to face while being in a successful band. They toured a lot in support of *Still Standing*, and were on the road constantly with 175 tour dates that year. During that time Lee's son, who was only seven months old, had a medical emergency that required him to have a liver transplant. Lee said he would finish playing a gig with Exile, and they would take the tour bus and drop him off at whatever airport was closest so he could fly back home to be with his family faster after the show. The rest of them would drive the many hours back home on the bus, just like they always did. Up until that point he had never missed a gig, and that year he missed 25. When his son's condition worsened, he and his family moved into a Ronald McDonald House to await an organ transplant. No one knew how long Lee would be gone, so they came up with a creative solution: they recorded Lee's parts and played along with them in his absence during their shows. They always explained to the crowd what they were doing and why, and it never failed to win the audience over. Through all the stress of playing every weekend, then taking leave to care for his sick child, no one in Exile contributed to making that stress any worse for him. Quite to the contrary, Lee said he never had a doubt that it wasn't ok with Steve, Sonny, Paul or Mark for him to go home at a moment's notice to take care of his family.

I failed to mention previously that the nickname the guys have for themselves is "The Exile Brothers." They aren't just a bunch of guys in a band together, they are brothers. Lee and Paul both got to experience first-hand just what it meant to have their Exile brothers help them out during their time of need. Those stressful situations made it clear what it meant to be an Exile brother - what was good for one was good for all. Lee said that due to those experiences together, those four guys will always be his friends, and he would do anything for them. It is precisely that feeling of brotherhood that has contributed to Exile's overall longevity, even though so many band members have come and gone through the years. There is something truly special about being in Exile, whether it's during the good times or the bad. And almost inconceivably, things were once again looking up for them.

Some of their fondest memories from those days are from when they toured with the Oak Ridge Boys. They always had fun and shared a lot of laughter playing good-natured pranks on the Oaks. For one of their shows together they played Caesar's Palace in Las Vegas. On this occasion, Exile convinced the management at Caesar's to let them wear the Roman sentinel costumes that the employees wore. They came marching out onstage during the Oaks' set, and they looked so silly in their Roman helmets and costumes that everyone fell apart laughing. The Oaks were always good sports, and they were never afraid of a little fun and good humor. On another night, Paul Martin rented an Elvis costume and came out on stage to surprise the Oaks during their set. This time, and without hardly missing a beat, the Oaks went into an Elvis medley that nearly brought the house down. The Oak Ridge Boys were true professionals, a great group of guys, and most importantly, they were good friends during Exile's many ups and downs. They definitely made life on the road more fun. Touring with the Oaks exposed more and more people to Exile's new songs, and most assuredly helped them to rise once again to the top of the charts.

The next single Exile released was a song written by Sonny LeMaire and fellow musician and songwriter, Randy Sharp, entitled "Nobody's Talking." That song was a departure in that it featured Sonny by himself on lead vocals, and it went all the way to #2. Exile was once again hitting a groove that really resonated with folks. After going from thinking the band was finished to having two top-ten hits, this was perhaps the best feeling yet. Together, they were conscious of each achievement. It is a fact that success cannot truly be appreciated without failure, gain without loss. They were proud yet humbled by their accomplishments. They had all worked so hard to make this thing work, and they truly appreciated just how far they had come. Exile's music once again found its home with audiences and their fans.

The last single from *Still Standing* was a ballad called "Yet," also written by Sonny and Randy Sharp. Sonny was again featured on lead vocals, and it was a sweet, seemingly simple song that it made it to #7 on the charts. On the surface it is about a girl who doesn't love a boy just yet, but I think it means much more:

1ST VERSE

When she says she doesn't love me

Anybody else might be upset

But to me it doesn't matter

'Cause all that really means is she doesn't love me yet

CHORUS

I keep on believin' she's gonna love me

I keep on tryin' she's gonna love me

She's gonna love me yet

BRIDGE

It's gonna take a lot of patience

It's gonna take a little time

If I wait I'm certain

Someday she'll be mine

3RD VERSE

You can say it's crazy

And it's something that someday I will regret

But when she says she doesn't love me

What she really means to say is she doesn't love me yet

This song perfectly illustrates the indefatigable spirit of Exile: that with patience and hard work, they could achieve the impossible. They had tweaked and re-invented their sound yet again, and it had worked. That lineup of guys breathed new life into Exile, and for that they should be commended. Their last single, "There You Go," went to #32, and that was just fine with them. Overall, *Still Standing* was a labor of love for the band, the music, and the fans. That album kept them going just when everyone thought they were through. It was and remains a true testament to their perseverance.

With the success of *Still Standing* on Arista records, they started writing new songs and went back into the studio to record their next album, *Justice*, in 1991. The first single, "Even Now," reflected the new sound they had cultivated together on the previous album. It was a melodic ballad that featured Paul's musical virtuosity. He is heard in the intro playing the mandolin, and he played steel guitar as well as lead guitar on that song. It was a top 20 hit that went to #16. They didn't know it then, but it would be the last song to chart for Exile in their many, many years of making music. The follow up singles, "Nothing At All" and "Somebody's Telling Her Lies" did not crack the top 100 in 1992. After an incredible run, their days of chart-topping hit singles were finally over.

Even though they weren't generating the #1 hits they once had, Exile still played over one hundred tour dates that year. One of the most memorable gigs that year was when they were asked to be a part of the opening ceremony of Euro Disney (now Disneyland Paris) in '92. It was a great honor for them to be asked to play, even though there was some controversy about the park itself at the time. The French in general and Parisians in particular, had very strong feelings about the "disneyfication" of their esteemed culture, and there were several protests against the opening of the park. Regardless, the guys went to Paris and performed their songs and had a great time. The opportunity to play the opening of Euro Disney was the chance of a lifetime, and overall it was a wonderful experience for them.

In 1993, Exile played their 30-year reunion at the Kentucky Horse Park in Lexington. Original and former band members Buzz Cornelison, Billy Luxon, Mike Howard, Mack Davenport, Bernie Faulkner, and J.P. Pennington all came out that night to celebrate the 30th anniversary of the band and join them onstage. The incredible

Bluegrass legend, Bill Monroe, opened up the festivities for them. They had a special party for the members of their fan club at the Campbell House, which was run by their old friend Jerry Morse. By all accounts the reunion was a huge success, and everyone had a great time. It was wonderful to get new and old band members together all in one place, and play the songs they all knew and loved. They celebrated 30 years of music that night, but the guys in the current lineup knew a big change was in the air. The magic, it seems, was finally gone.

By the end of summer '93 they made the decision to end the band. Sonny called a band meeting at their hotel while they were on the road. According to Steve Goetzman, Sonny said, "Let's give it up while we still have some dignity." It was a tough decision, but the rest of the guys reluctantly agreed. It was time. They finished out all their tour dates, and in February 1994, Exile played their last show. After all this time, and many near-endings for the band, they finally decided to call it quits for good. They said goodbye, and each went his separate way. It was a shock, an adjustment, and a period of sadness. It was the end of a great band, and the end of an era for those Kentucky musicians. They did, however, release another album called *Latest & Greatest* in 1995, which included the newer hits "I Can't Get Close Enough," "Keep it in the Middle of the Road," "Nobody's Talking," and "Yet," as well as older hits like "Woke Up in Love," and "Give Me One More Chance." The album contained some completely new material as well, like the single "How Bad Can It Be," and gave their fans a great mix of the old and new country hits. Of course, no greatest hits album would be complete without "Kiss you All Over." *Latest & Greatest* was a nice way for them to wrap up a decades' worth of songs.

For the remainder of the 90s, the Exile guys pretty much lost track of one another. Steve Goetzman had moved down to Nashville, and he went on to manage artists like Steve Wariner, Eric Heatherly, and journalist, music critic and author, Alanna Nash. Sonny LeMaire, too, had moved to Nashville, where he continued writing songs. He penned a huge hit with co-writer Marc Beeson for Restless Heart called "When She Cries," which was a crossover hit that made it to the top of both the country and pop charts. He had another hit in 2002 with "Beautiful Mess" for

Diamond Rio, with co-writers Shane Minor and Clay Mills. Paul Martin went on to play with Kathy Mattea and the Oak Ridge Boys. Mark Jones became Entertainment Director for the famous Wildhorse Saloon in Nashville, and later got into the artist management side of the music business. Lee Carroll left the music world entirely to go into business with his brother in Louisville, KY. Together they opened a very successful Papa Johns franchise, and Lee moved away to Pennsylvania. He didn't play the keyboards again for ten long years. For him, those years were exhausting both physically and emotionally, and the grind really took the joy out of playing music. Surprisingly, somehow, life indeed went on for all of them without Exile.

In 1995, however, J.P. and Les had had enough of trying to make it as solo artists, so they got together and decided they wanted to revive the band. The other guys were busy with the new lives they'd made for themselves, so J.P. and Les hired a backing band and went out together to play all their greatest Exile hits. They had Jimmy Ellison on drums, Jeff Watson on bass, and Jason Witt on keyboards. They both had sung lead vocals on many of the hit country songs, so it worked out well for them. They continued playing gigs together until 2006, when Les departed once again, and J.P. continued on until 2008. For the rest of the 90s, though, many years passed and the guys hardly spoke to one another, if at all. I, too, felt the rift, not just from the band, whom I had known almost all my life, but also from my dad. They went into the new millennium practically estranged. For most of them, their Exile days seemed to be behind them for good.

THE 00s TO PRESENT

The 90s saw the dissolution of several Exile lineups, and even though J.P. continued to play under that name, he was the only member from the days when they had hit records together. Then, in 2007, tragedy struck. Their old friend and road manager, Raymond Patrick, had a terrible motorcycle wreck while out riding a friend's Harley Road King on the Mountain Parkway. He was in a coma for six weeks, then in the hospital for three months. His good friend Doug Breeding called up each of the guys and told them what had happened. They were all very concerned and wanted to do something to help. Doug had another popular Lexington bar by this time called the Blue Moon, and he and Sonny tossed around the idea that maybe they could play a benefit to help Raymond with his hospital expenses. They had played together as Doug and Sonny many, many years ago, and they thought perhaps they could revive their old act for one evening. Then, one day, Doug, Sonny and J.P. were in the car together going to visit Raymond in the hospital when the idea for an Exile reunion came about. They thought that, just maybe, they could get J.P., Les, Steve, Marlon and Sonny (the original country lineup) back together for one night only. Keep in mind that many of these guys hadn't spoken to each other, much less played together, for the better part of two decades, since Marlon left in 1986. Sonny made some calls, and lo and behold, they all said yes. They were getting the band back together. According to J.P. there were two main reasons for the show: 1) They all loved Raymond and wanted to do whatever they could to help him out, and 2) They all really missed each other.

In early 2008 the old lineup started rehearsing together. They were admittedly a bit rusty, and it took a little while to break the ice and get comfortable with one another again. There were some hurt feelings, in addition to some long and not-so-forgotten grudges to get past, yet slowly but surely things started once again to click. In March of 2008, on St. Patrick's Day, they played the Exile reunion show at the Blue Moon. J.P. said it was one of the best nights ever, out of all their many nights of playing together. Not to mention the fact that the place was packed, and about 95% of the crowd was people they knew, including their die-hard fans who had been with them from their earliest days. Doug Breeding said there were some young people in the audience that night who didn't know exactly know who Exile was, but as soon as they started playing those kids realized they knew those hit songs, and couldn't believe their good fortune to get to see them play. Once again, Exile had come home and found the outpouring of love and support that had always been there for them. There was so much home-town love in the room, and they got to see just how much people still cared about them and their music. They all looked at each other and thought "This is still really good." It was really emotional for everyone involved. That night was the catalyst that brought them all back together.

They've been playing together ever since. They're a little older, a little wiser, and a bit more mellow, but they've still got it. Playing music is everything to these guys. J.P. even said that playing together now is more fun than it ever was, and that they are better than they've ever been. I think the reason for that feeling is that they are back home where they belong, on the stage, doing what they love. According to Les:

There's a camaraderie between us all, a chemistry. We care about the music, we care about our live shows. We've always been concerned about doing the best show we can do. After being together as long as we have, what makes the band work is the chemistry and professionalism.

In 2012, Trace Adkins recorded a version of "Kiss You All Over" with them. The guys were thrilled that such a huge country star would be interested in doing a cover of one of their songs. It has yet to be released, but that song still has the magic it always did. Marlon admitted:

Even today when we play "Kiss", there's nothing unique about the C, F chord progression, but when they hear those first chords, the crowd just goes nuts. Musically it doesn't make any sense, but it just works.

Exile's longevity can be perhaps summed up in much the same way: it may not make a lot of sense, but it definitely works. Richard Young of

The Kentucky Headhunters once told Marlon that "Everybody wanted to be in Exile, or a band just like it. They were the coolest." Said Marlon:

> Coming from those guys, you could tell they were really appreciative of what we'd done. And it always makes you feel good to know that other bands feel that way, because sometimes in the past, we've often felt like we were maybe overlooked to a certain extent. It's really nice to hear that we influenced other bands. I think that we were an innovative band through the years.

Exile's legacy lives on in their music. Steve Goetzman recently joked that "A lot of people call it 'marquee value;' I call it luck." They have made a lasting contribution to pop, rock and country music in general, and to Kentucky music in specific, and for that reason they are being honored with induction to the Kentucky Music Hall of Fame in April 2013, right alongside their good friends the Kentucky Headhunters, and other talented Kentucky artists. Welcome home boys; we missed you.

WHERE ARE THEY NOW

J.P. Pennington, Steve Goetzman, Marlon Hargis, Sonny LeMaire and Les Taylor are still touring together and playing shows like Woodsongs Old Time Radio Hour and the Grand Ol' Opry. In 2011 they released their first new music in over twenty years, an EP entitled *People Get Ready*. They are currently working on a live CD/DVD recorded at the Franklin Theatre in Franklin, TN. It is scheduled to be released end of summer 2013.

Lee Carroll is in a music/art collective called Tin Can Buddha in Pennsylvania. They are a rotating group of artists and musicians who play together for the sheer love of making art and playing music. Mark Jones is a contributing member as well. Lee also sits in with half a dozen bands in the area, and sometimes plays with jazz guitarist Bruce Lewis.

Buzz Cornelison worked for many years at his family's business, Bybee Pottery, and has kept his love for the theatre alive by working on many productions for the Actors' Guild of Lexington. He went on to join the Board of Directors of the new Performing Arts Center in Richmond. He then left that position   and is currently working with the Upward Bound Program at Eastern Kentucky University, which helps low income and rural youths to stay in school and go on to college.

Mack Davenport plays music for fun to this day. He and Mike Howard still get together on regularly and jam. Sometimes they play Southern rock with a couple of other guys. He also runs into Buzz Cornelison every few months.

Bernie Faulkner said he helped a young up-and comer named Billy Ray Cyrus when he was just starting out, and he has helped other musicians learn the ins and outs of the music industry. He currently has his own record label in Nashville, 78rpm, where he recently signed vocalist Carla Jo Carr and world champion finger style guitarist Wesley Crider.

Mark Gray lives with his wife in Nashville, and he continues to write songs.

Mike Howard is retired from the post office, and now plays in a band in Richmond called Prime Cut. They do covers of bands like Chicago, The Temptations, and Blood, Sweat & Tears.

Jeff Hunt finally gave up life on the road to stay home and raise his two girls. He still loves rock-n-roll.

Bobby Johns is Director of Admissions at a medical college in FL, but his great love is taking in rescue animals and volunteering at local shelters. As of this writing he had 28 adopted dogs and cats.

Mark Jones decided to go into the management side of music, and he got a job as road manager for Chely Wright and Sara Evans. He now works with Clarence Spalding at Spalding Entertainment as manager for Chely Wright.

Bill Luxon sold J Sutter's Mill after 20 successful years of business. He then went into foodservice distribution, and he is currently Manager of Sales Development at one of the top three foodservice companies in the nation. He and his wife Margaret Jo recently celebrated their 30th wedding anniversary.

Paul Martin started playing with Marty Stuart and the Fabulous Superlatives in February 2008, and they went on to win a Grammy for Hummingbyrd in 2011. He is married with four children, and his family plays together as The Martin Family Circus when he isn't on tour with Marty.

Billy Moore still roadies and does front of house for Montgomery Gentry.

Raymond Patrick left the music business and went on to become a contractor, and he especially likes to build log homes.

Clarence Spalding is President of Spalding Entertainment, and he went on to work with hit-makers Rascal Flatts, Brooks & Dunn, Jason Aldean and Kix Brooks. He previously served as

Chairman of the Country Music Association, and Director of the Academy of Country Music.

Nicole LeMaire lives on the Lower East Side and works in Midtown, Manhattan. About six years ago her boyfriend, Steven, flew her dad up for a surprise birthday party. She had complained to him that her dad had never visited her in all the years she had lived in New York, so Steven set out to remedy the situation. The night of the party, Nicole and her dad had a heart-to-heart that changed their relationship forever. She forgave him for being gone when she was a kid, and he forgave her for being an angry teen/ young adult/older adult. They repaired their relationship at about the same time as Exile repaired theirs. Funny how life works out, isn't it?